"One does not become enlightened by imagining figures of light, but by making the darkness conscious."

Carl Gustav Jung

OVERCOME ADDICTION

365 Inspirations For Recovery

Also By C.W. V. Straaten

The Addiction Recovery Workbook:
A 7-step Master Plan For Lasting Recovery

The Addiction Recovery Journal:
366 Days of Transformation, Writing & Reflection

Shifting Attention: The Curious Tale Of Addiction:
And The Magical Art Of Recovery

Disclaimer

This book is not intended to act as a substitute for medical advice or treatment. Any person with a condition requiring medical attention should consult a qualified medical practitioner or suitable therapist. The information provided in this book is stated to be truthful and consistent, in that any liability, in terms of inattention or otherwise, by any usage or abuse of any policies, processes, or directions contained within is the solitary and utter responsibility of the recipient reader. Under no circumstances will any legal responsibility or blame be held against the publisher for any reparation, damages, or monetary loss due to the information herein, either directly or indirectly.

OVERCOME ADDICTION

365 Inspirations For Recovery

C.W. V. STRAATEN

Instagram: become_recovery

The Alexander Publishing House
2020

Declaration Of Intent

This book is created with the intention to help you with daily recovery. To help you find the inner light of your awareness. And to help you heal, wake up from the deceitful lies and spells of addiction. My books are dedicated with love to all those who suffer from their cravings, to all those who are about to give up, to all who've found the courage to choose for recovery, and to all who're extending a helping hand to those who suffer from addiction.

Thank You Note

Dear Reader,

Thanks for purchasing this book.

As a little thank you gift, we have created a guided meditation for addiction recovery. Simply send an email to cw.vanstraaten@yahoo.com

Title the email "365 Inspirations"

And we will send you the meditation for free.

Introduction

What always fascinated me about life, is the chance to turn it all around in a moment. A decision away from radical change. Addiction is a spell, a lengthy and clever deception, a destructive comfort zone that becomes more unpenetrable each time you act out its cycle. Then, the irrational becomes wisdom and lies the truth. It's a reality of continuous craving. Of running around, faster and faster, but never, ever to arrive. Never to belong. Addiction has but one finish line, one despondent goal: total destruction. It steals your awareness, your inner truth. To eradicate the light, because only in darkness fear can live. Only in darkness, the monster can feed itself. Only in the darkness lies can pose as the truth. It's a realm where destruction is the deceitful king.

What to do then, because I feel so small, so powerless in these vast fields of gloom.

Darkness is the absence of light. There is no dark vs. light, only different levels of light. To go up, to higher levels, you have to increase your awareness. Your inner light. To align with your true self. To wake up. If you read these words, you've made the decision to move away from the 'dark'. To move away from addiction. And to step into the bright fields of recovery. It's a journey of waking up.

Personally, I have no preference when it comes to recovery methods. What I believe to be most important is to keep shining the healing light of awareness on your addiction, your inner wounds, habitually, and with determination. To make recovery a daily practice. A daily habit that in time can transcend the addiction cycle. Whether that's through twelve steps meeting, rehab, therapy, or self-coaching. However, asking for help, sharing your secrets, consulting a professional, it's always recommended. It makes the journeyer simpler, less alone, more in-depth, and meaningful.

This book, just like my other one-year book *The Addiction Recovery Journal*, will help you to make recovery a daily habit. These 365 Inspirations are mainly texts from the other books I've written on addiction. And also relevant quotes from other authors and new written content. The first part of this book is mostly about addiction recovery. In the latter stages, I have also included many other texts on self-growth and spiritual growth. Because recovery is about more than just your addiction. It's about dealing with and ultimately healing your inner wounds. And living a life that's in agreement with your authentic self, with your truly chosen values. On the seventh day of each week, I've included a guided question. To help you reflect on your recovery process.

I want to finish this introduction with a text from my book *Shifting Attention*:

Realize what there is to gain if you stop giving time, attention, resources, energy to such a destructive habit. What life awaits you after moving away from addiction. After breaking your agreement, there will be Freedom. Time to walk into the land of possibilities. To feel the touch of a lover, hear the whispers of a new spring, to see the awakening of a new beginning in everything that surrounds you. To reclaim the I am again and walk forward with the strength of character and an exhilaration sense of beingness. Realize you've come here, to this earth, to this one life, with a purpose, a calling. There is a song waiting within you. You have the voice, the being, the qualities to sing that song. To follow your music. Your calling. To make your life a ride of joy, a ride of discovery, a ride of creation, a ride of love. To make this experience truly worthwhile. Don't play the level of craving over and over again. It's not worth it. There is life after addiction. There is life after recovery. There is so much more out there for you to discover. Embrace it. Embrace the new. Empty the old. The beliefs, the stories, the thoughts that clearly don't work. Replace them. Write a new chapter. Walk a new path. Find your song.

And start singing it.

I wish your peace, progress, and all the best,

C.W. V. Straaten
Buenos Aires 2020

Daily Recovery Inspirations

If you want to focus on becoming free from addiction & commit to recovery every day, follow my instagram account. With a recovery inspiration every day.

Instagram: become_recovery

https://www.instagram.com/become_recovery/.

Or you can search for C.W. V. Straaten.

DAY 1

THE TIME IS NOW

Now is the time to break free from the isolated nights of addictions. The suffering of relapses. The suffocating lies. All these secrets, followed by intense loneliness. These will be memories from the past. The time has come to break out. To be you. To be that person you came here to be. Your dreams, your hopes, and talents: they're not gone. They're still here. You can still sing your song. Reclaim your I am. Reclaim your voice. Reclaim your song. You are more than an addiction. And you are even more than recovery. You are loved eternally. And the light within you, the light around you will set you free. A new path is awaiting you. A new direction awakened. Claim it. Liberate the old. And welcome your new life. The time is now.

DAY 2

What triggers you to start your addiction cycle? And what is the reward of your addiction cycle? Why this need to escape, to numb, to run away from the present moment, to go into hiding from the *here* and *now*. What is so scary, so radically frightening that you rather run a thousand miles than to face it? What is it, exactly, that drives you to utterly irrational behavior, to repeat a destructive pattern over and over and over and over again?

DAY 3

I AM IN RECOVERY

Reality is a mirror of who you are. As long as you identify yourself as an addict, that's the reality you are living in. This identification can happen either consciously or unconsciously. It makes no difference, the end result is the same. You attract who you are. The first step to lasting recovery is to stop the agreement with addiction. To no longer identify yourself as an addiction.

To declare: *I am in recovery.*

And when you make that declaration, everything that happens next is part of a recovery journey. Even a relapse becomes a part of that journey.

DAY 4

"A human being has so many skins inside, covering the depths of the heart. We know so many things, but we don't know ourselves! Why, thirty or forty skins or hides, as thick and hard as an ox's or bear's, cover the soul. Go into your own ground and learn to know yourself there." - Meister Eckhart

DAY 5

LANDSCAPE OF REALITY

Fundamental change is possible. Even in surprisingly short periods of time. The reality of addiction you are living in now can soon be transcended. A transformed life awaits you when you break the agreement with addiction. When you stop identifying yourself with addiction. What you focus on expands. So bring the attention of your being to recovery. Fundamentally stop focusing your attention on addiction. But focus on a new decision.

Focus on the declaration, *I am in recovery.* It will change your landscape of reality radically.

DAY 6

"If we look fear in the eye, it always diminishes.
It shrinks when we shine the light.
Bit by bit we are waking up to the truth:

There are no monsters under the bed."

Zen Mirrors

DAY 7

Write down five of your most common addiction thoughts. Then rephrase them in an empowering statement. For example, *I will always fall back to addictive behavior* vs. *I am no longer in agreement with my addictive behavior and even a relapse is part of my recovery journey.*

Day 8

Pattern Of Addiction

To start this journey to recovery, you have to observe what's running you. Deconstruct addiction so to say. Make it small, compartmentalize it. The first step is to discover your pattern of addiction. From point zero until the moment you are heavily drinking, or gambling, or whatever your addictive behavior is.

With what thoughts or sensations is the pattern starting?

Where are you when it starts?

What triggers your addiction?

Day 9

It's almost impossible to see another reality when you are caught up in the claws of addiction. Like it's hard for someone in depression to observe and appreciate the colors of flowers. The path for an addict goes from craving to relief. Then there is a temporary pleasure. When the pleasure ends, there is suffering. And to numb this suffering the craving comes in again. It's a vicious circle, that seems like an endless running wheel. Continuing over and over and over again.

DAY 10

LESSONS TO LEARN

We are here to learn lessons in life. As long as we don't grasp the lesson of our current level, we can't ascend to another level. And life can be a harsh teacher. The first few times we don't learn, the consequences are often small, hardly noticeable. But the longer we ignore the lessons, the heavier the consequences will be. When you drink a few too many, the consequence can be a hangover. And maybe an embarrassing rant to a friend. When the drinking begins to start every day, consequences will increase. Step by step. Heavier and heavier. So it is with every addiction. It starts innocently. A visit to a casino with friends. Watching pornography as a teenager. Trying out drugs as a young adult. But then slowly but surely, it takes a downhill path. A path of destruction.

DAY 11

The lesson is obvious: you can't ignore your inner pain. A temporary release is not the solution. In a higher state of consciousness dealing with your inner pains becomes easier. When you are in addiction, eternally running away from your pain, becoming whole is impossible. You need to disrupt the wheel. You need to stop this pattern: craving, relief, pleasure, suffering, craving.

DAY 12

THE MIRROR

Life reflects the person who is looking at her.

When you look at life, know that she stares back. Who you are, is what you see. Stop trying to change the mirror. Out there nothing brings fulfillment. All that's brought to you is a mere reflection. It's life bouncing back. The thoughts. The being. Go within. For there's someone looking at the mirror. Change him and all else will change along. What once was winter is now the time to rest and reflect. What once was the reason for sorrow, now is an element of flow.

DAY 13

Higher levels will be experienced on rare occasions. So that makes it possible that even when all seems lost, you might experience luminous feelings of hope. And from that feeling of hope receive inspired thoughts that can eventually lead to recovery.

The impact of higher states is enormous. Ten minutes in a state of joy can turn a bad day into a good one. Feeling the sensations of absolute love, of absolute truth, can be the inspiration for life-changing decisions.

DAY 14

WEEKLY REFLECTION

Describe the moment that you realized you had an addiction.

Day 15

The Investigation

Stand up against this destructive guest in your house of being. In your life. Investigate your addiction. Expose it. Stop living at its mercy. Stop the fear of addiction. By getting to know it through and through. Stand up against uncontrolled behavior. It is you who owns your life. Who owns your decisions and actions. Discover all the lies and tricks addiction tells you. Knowledge will be your weapon, and with this weapon, you can start to defeat your addiction.

And the knowledge comes from investigation.

Day 16

Start your investigation by writing down your addiction pattern. Start with the first moment where the craving starts, until the addiction takes over full control. Write down all the thoughts that belong to your addictive behavior. Write down the lies and tricks it uses to make you relapse. Find out everything. Addiction is a victory for uncontrolled behavior. To counter this, you need to become aware of your thoughts. Of your sensations. Of your actions.

Awareness will set you free.

DAY 17

INTERRUPT ADDICTIVE BEHAVIOR

How can you interrupt your addictive behavior?

The first step is realization. To realize your *power*: You have control over your own life. You are the emperor. When you embrace this self-responsibility thousands of possibilities appear on your landscape. Addiction doesn't need to run your life forever. There are thousands, no millions, no trillions of options to stop the pattern of your addiction. To move away from the craving. To walk on the enlightened path of recovery. To live a life of joy, of freedom, of abundance and happiness.

And that journey starts by taking small steps. It starts with taking back your control.

DAY 18

What helps you forward, besides the weapon of knowledge, is your inner spirit. The light within. The faith that can move mountains. Know that the universe, a higher power is on your side. Whenever we take a journey away from the destruction, into the light: the universe will move to help you succeed.

DAY 19

OCEANS OF FREEDOM

"To live is to change,
and to be perfect
is to have changed often."
John Henry Newman

DAY 20

What is your reason for this journey of recovery? Why do you want to overcome your addiction? What awaits you if you quit drinking? Or quit smoking? Or quit watching pornography? Create compelling reasons that lead you forward on this journey. What is waiting at the end of the horizon? Write down a list of your biggest why's for overcoming your addiction. And keep repeating these reasons in your mind. By writing them down every day. Or repeating them mentally. Know why you are doing this. Why you are choosing this path of recovery. It's good to realize that you will gain extra energy, extra time, and probably extra money when you overcome your addiction. Think about that for a second. It's not just a little bit of extra energy and time. We are talking about oceans of freedom. What could you do with all these extra resources? What is possible when you are no longer in the reality of addiction?

DAY 21

WEEKLY REFLECTION

Write down a list of at least five reasons why you absolutely want to overcome your addiction for good.

Day 22

A New Future

Create a new future. You don't need to wait for that. The future doesn't start tomorrow. Or after you have overcome your addiction. It starts now. With a small step in a new direction. With a small step into the light of a brighter future. So start dreaming today. Create compelling dreams you are absolutely believing in. Create a short term vision. A life that you could live within three or six months. And a long term vision. One year from now. And five years from now. Make it compelling. Make it something energizing.

Make it so fantastic that you want to jump out of bed to realize it.

Day 23

"Some people, in order to discover God, read books. But there is a great book: the very appearance of created things. Look above you! Look below you! Read it. God, whom you want to discover, never wrote that book with ink. Instead, He set before your eyes the things that He had made. Can you ask for a louder voice than that?"

Augustine of Hippo

Day 24

REWRITE THE PATTERN

You feel that craving again. And the circle starts again. Because it will be there again. Addiction has been your comfort zone. And it won't give up so easily. But remember that it isn't so strong as it appears to be. It is just a pattern. And that pattern can be broken.

There are thoughts and these thoughts can be rewritten. There are sensations, and these sensations can be released. And there are actions, and these actions can be done differently.

Day 25

Even if the sorrows stay, new realizations will lighten your burden and the burden of your fellow man. Of future generations. For no information ever goes wasted. Then immerse yourself in something good and together we will raise.

We will say, yes, it is but a distant memory. Chains will be gone. And the rewards you will reap are not small in joy and inner wealth.

Day 26

The Drunkard

"Gifts, smiles, words.

We hide behind borders.

Of thoughts.

Of memories.

What flowers do you hide inside?"

Zen Mirrors

Day 27

""What are you doing there?" he said to the drunkard, whom he found settled down in silence before a collection of empty bottles and also a collection of full bottles. "I am drinking," replied the drunkard, with a lugubrious air. "Why are you drinking?" demanded the little prince. "So that I may forget," replied the drunkard. "Forget what?" inquired the little prince, who already was sorry for him. "Forget that I am ashamed," the drunkard confessed, hanging his head. "Ashamed of what?" insisted the little prince, who wanted to help him. "Ashamed of drinking!" The drunkard brought his speech to an end and shut himself up in an impregnable silence. And the little prince went away, puzzled."

From *The Little Prince*, by Antoine de Saint–Exupéry

DAY 28

Write down at least five reasons why you're addictive behavior is irrational.

DAY 29

THE NATURE OF YOUR OWN REALITY IS MALLEABLE

To become more awakened to the actual nature of reality, it is important to educate yourself in the different levels of vibrational energy. As you would understand, gambling your whole salary in one evening is a different state of consciousness, then walking on the beach with your loved one. Or drinking a bottle of vodka to forget your emotional pain, is a different state than getting a relaxing massage. Everything consists of energy. The nature of your own reality is malleable.

DAY 30

Everyone sees life differently. The stories you tell yourself, determine how you perceive the physical reality around you. For some people, addiction is not part of their everyday lives. Some addicts recover and never return to their addictive behavior. Others relapse over and over again. How do you get out of that vicious cycle? What is reality? Is there one reality everybody is experiencing? Or do you have more power than you think? Are your thoughts creating the reality you are experiencing? Food for thought, definitely. The beginning of fundamental change is to see addiction for what it is. To stop giving it so much importance. To shift attention.

DAY 31

AUTHENTICITY

The happiness we all seek lies in living an authentic life. Expressing yourself truthfully, serving your true purpose here on earth. From your authentic self, you can love truly, create truly, live truly. But as long as you are attaching yourself to deep untrue uncertainties you keep fighting a battle. Running around in circles, chasing your own tail. Until you realize that the answer was, is, and always will be within, you are stuck in a rat race you can never win. You are living within your own belief system. Life is a mirror. If you don't release your trauma's, the resentment, your limiting beliefs, the mirror will never truly change. Not a multimillion-dollar mansion, not a stunning partner, and no world recognition could change that.

DAY 32

"There are words inside you.
They long for expression.
To what hour do you wait?
Which moment is good enough?
Don't wait no longer, to sing your song."

Zen Mirrors

DAY 33

PERCEPTION

"If the doors of perception were cleansed
every thing would appear to man as it is,
Infinite.
For man has closed himself up,
till he sees all things thro' narrow chinks of his cavern."

William Blake

DAY 34

During my recovery journey, I've learned many new things but none of them had such a profound impact on my life as creating a morning ritual. It is transforming to start the day by taking control of your morning. Instead of Facebook feeds or news channels claiming your attention, you control your time and prepare yourself for the day.

This habit alone, which could take as long as fifteen minutes, can be a game-changer during your recovery.

DAY 35

Write down an empowering morning routine (minimal 15 minutes) you could try out for a week.

DAY 36

SECRET PAY-OFF

The first step towards this radical change is awareness of the problem itself. We wouldn't indulge in any behavior if there isn't an emotional pay-off. We always try to help ourselves. To do what feels the absolute best to us in every given moment. Either you try to avoid pain or gain pleasure. And the need to avoid pain is usually bigger than the need for pleasure. So what is your secret pay-off for your addictive behavior?

DAY 37

The dictionary gives the following definition of a comfort zone:

a situation in which you feel comfortable and in which your ability and determination are not being tested.

So what is comfortable if you're stuck in a reality of addiction? Exactly, the way of least resistance: feeling relieved through a substance or certain actions. What is outside the comfort zone, thus where are your abilities and determination tested? By resisting that craving, or better still, transcending the craving.

DAY 38

PRESENCE

Feel your body, feel your emotions, feel your breathing, feel your heart. Zoom out. Zoom out again. And again. Become the observer of your thoughts, of your life, of life in general. Do it today. Do it even now. Take five minutes, or ten minutes and simply be. Sit down, lie down or walk slowly around. Open your eyes and observe. Open your ears and hear. Open your heart and feel. Even when thoughts are rushing in, observe them. Detach yourself from your worries, your image, and all the has to's. And simply perceive.

DAY 39

Write down your addiction patterns but with a different end. Instead of letting it end in addictive behavior, end it in something great, funny, joyful, playful, creative, something extremely different. So for example, drinking your first shot of vodka, becomes calling a friend, depositing money on a sports betting site, becomes loaning microcredit on Kiva, etc. If you want the best experience: visualize the new pattern after you've written it down.

For maximum benefit keep repeating this exercise on a daily basis.

DAY 40

TAKE A BREATH

"What is life more than the passing of time?

Sit down for a minute.

Take a breath.

Look outside.

Look within.

Discover the miracles for yourself.

And then the passing of time will never, ever be just the passing of time again."

Zen Mirrors

DAY 41

Visualize one of your addiction patterns. Do this sitting down with your eyes closed, or lying on bed. Meditation music can help with this exercise. Then interrupt the addiction pattern several times. For example, instead of going to the fridge to get a beer and drink it. Go to the fridge, get a beer, open it, and put it down the toilet. Or instead of buying a six-pack beer, buy a bottle of your favorite soda. You can do the visualization sitting or lying down in a comfortable position, and if you'd like, with music. It can take anywhere from 3 to 20 minutes. Or longer if that feels right to you.

DAY 42

Write down the thoughts, the worries, the fears, the doubts that are running through your mind. Release yourself from the weight of it.

DAY 43

HIGHER POWER

There is an incredible power surrounding us. Some may call it God, Presence, Allah, All-Knowing, or The Universe. It's not in the name, it's in what it stands for. Remember that this Higher Power is available to all of us. Religious or non-religious. Prayers can be extremely helpful in ascending from addiction. There is no how-to, however. It's very personal, and different for everyone. If you pray with the genuine intention to ask for guidance and help for your recovery journey, you can be assured that this help and guidance will be given to you. Love heals all, conquers all. If you have the genuine intention and determination to ascend from lower levels of consciousness, the Universe will grant you the help you need. But this, of course, is a matter of faith. For the readers who are too skeptical to do this exercise, you can also connect with your Higher Self. In a sense, asking yourself for guidance. But do remember, that what you've done so far, has only brought you a reality where addiction is present. To find a new path, you have to liberate the old.

DAY 44

"Love will find a way through paths where wolves fear to prey."
Lord Byron

Day 45

Huge Shift

A huge shift occurred when I, dog tired of the financial stress, and the senselessness of it all, traded the belief 'Gambling is the only way how I can recoup my losses' with 'If I gamble I am always, without exception, losing money in the end.' The shorter version was: Gambling equals losing money. I repeated this mantra so often to myself, in writing, in saying, in meditation, in prayer, hundreds, thousands of times. But more importantly, I took actions according to this new belief. I needed to face my financial debts and to find a way to make more money. Gambling equals losing money meant that at all costs gambling couldn't be a part of that new plan.

Day 46

"The journey to who you really are.

That's the only one.

It's all about letting go.

What's in your way to realize who you truly are?"

Zen Mirrors

Day 47

ROLE MODELS

Want some inspiration today?

Research other persons who overcame your addiction. Find stories on the internet who recovered from a drinking problem or overeating, etc. The benefit of this exercise is to realize that true and lasting change is possible. To realize there are people out there who have done what you would like to do. If you want to get the most out of this exercise, write down the lessons you can learn from these recovery stories.

Day 48

Remember, throughout this journey of recovery, throughout the journey of life: don't be too hard for yourself.

Please don't.

A little love for yourself can go a long way. It is the announcement of a new dawn. I sincerely hope that some words in this book will help you to find that new dawn. To eventually stop addiction. Put an end to it. Find recovery. And then, find a new life. Your life.

DAY 49

What empowering beliefs do you have about yourself?

DAY 50

BE YOUR OWN FRIEND

Regret is a logical consequence of making the 'wrong' decisions in the past. Especially when these decisions became a pattern and created destruction. When you confront yourself with your past mistakes it's easy to fall into self-blame. It's good to feel these feelings. And to express them in a civilized way. But another part in this process is to take small steps towards making things better.

First of all, understand and accept that the journey of recovery is tough enough already. You don't need another enemy. You need a friend. So at the very least, be your own friend. Help yourself. And recognize the fact that deciding you want to quit your addiction and taking the small steps to do so is an enormous accomplishment. Every time someone decides to break destruction, it lights up the world.

DAY 51

"There is no path to happiness:
happiness is the path."

Buddha

Day 52

Addiction is a victory for uncontrolled behavior. A good counteraction to addiction is to set intentions, and to follow through. To gain back control. This can be done with very small, trivial seeming actions. Saying, I am going to drink a glass of water. And then doing it. Or, I am going to water the plants, and then do it.

The way you do one thing is the way you do everything.

Step by step take back control of your life. If you can do it with the small things. The big things will follow soon.

Day 53

"This Universal Life, according to Zen, pillars the heaven, supports the earth, glorifies the sun and moon, gives voice to thunder, tinges clouds, adorns the pasture with flowers, enriches the field with harvest, gives animals beauty and strength. Therefore, Zen declares even a dead clod of earth to be imbued with the divine life."

Kaiten Nukariya

DAY 54

BLUE WATER

There will come a moment when you fully enjoy the fruits of your work and the safety of your outstanding character, a moment where you dance, have one of these rare, great conversations, or walk on a magnificent island with your loved one...

There, glancing over the blue water and feeling a tingling breeze on a sunny afternoon, you will stop for a moment. Realizing, without a single doubt, that all of the struggle, all of the pain and all of the tears have been worth it.

DAY 55

Write down a list of at least five self-care actions you can take immediately to help yourself if a relapse occurs.

It's important to calm down. To not fall into (too much) negative self-talk. Make actions easy and comfortable. It can be good to get out of your isolation (taking a walk, going to a friend, or loved one), or to rest well (shower, bath, or taking a long nap). You know yourself best, so write down a list of self-care actions that work for you.

Day 56

Write down five reasons why you and addiction are not a match any longer.

Day 57

Deeper Issues

Know that addiction numbs a deeper pain. Solving that inner issue is not a prerequisite for recovery. In fact, addiction is the act of running away from the real problems. So recovery is the first priority. From higher states of consciousness, it becomes much easier to deal with your inner wounds. When you are ready for it, the first step you can take to deal with your inner wounds is to become aware of what it is you're running away from. And you can find a good method, that feels safe and right to you, that can help you to deal with the pain.

Day 58

"Do not believe in anything simply because you have heard it. Do not believe in anything simply because it is spoken and rumored by many. Do not believe in anything simply because it is found written in your religious books. Do not believe in anything merely on the authority of your teachers and elders. Do not believe in traditions because they have been handed down for many generations. But after observation and analysis, when you find that anything agrees with reason and is conducive to the good and benefit of one and all, then accept it and live up to it."

Buddha

DAY 59

CHANGE YOUR IDENTITY

Become aware of what you're doing, how you're doing it and why you're doing it. Rewrite the story. Change your identity. Because your thoughts and actions are in alignment with your core beliefs. In alignment with who you believe you are. Shrug of the old I am an addict which (subconsciously) runs your life: take back control of your thoughts, and create a new you. Make use of the levels of consciousness to know what kind of beliefs, thoughts and actions you need to create a better life. And commit yourself to transformation. Change the inside and soon the outside will reflect that change in identity. Life is a mirror.

DAY 60

"If you worry about some issue for weeks,

For months, for years,

Maybe this is a good time, to blow the worries in the wind,

Let The Universe help you.

Give the issue faith. Let it disappear from your mind.

And go on."

Zen Mirrors

Day 61

More Than Tiny Little Fools

Already we feel there are many with us.

From dark to light. From low to high.

In us are many secret lands, with one we can heal the other.

So let us be more than shame. And more than worry.

Let us then grow above the craving.

With courage, compassion, intellect, enthusiasm, and love.

Find the better within.

We are more than tiny, little fools.

Seek high to heal the low.

Day 62

"Thousands and thousands of words full of tears. It was in those darkest moments, when the thunder of my drinking problem set me on fire, that I somehow found a way to write. To push out all my anger, lost dreams and fear into the tiny pages of my notebook. When, many drinks later, I started to find sobriety it was to those blank pages I returned. My pen functions as the bridge between my thoughts and the white lined paper. While writing, for the first time in a long, dark period, I found a sense of control. I found my sword against the drunken demons." - Joanne Edmund, *The Sobriety Journal*

DAY 63

What has life been trying to tell you over the past few years?

Day 64

POWERFUL STATEMENTS

Write down at least five statements that will help you during your recovery journey. For best benefits, write down these statements every day for the next 30 days. And repeat them out loud.
Examples:

There is so much more to life than the pain and suffering from addiction.

Addiction is a waste of my time.

Life in recovery is absolutely authentic for me.

Addiction is a lie, my spirit is the truth of recovery.

Only a fool waits for addiction to make him/her happy

Addiction is killing my energy for life, recovery is my new energy.

Day 65

"There are two ways of spreading light:
to be the candle or the mirror that receives it." - Edith Wharton

Day 66

Time

Does time exist the way we think it does? Seconds, hours, months, they come and go. Slowly, fast. Seemingly an advancement of numbers. Year 19. AD, 1672, 7.10 AM, June 7th. We are in the middle, of these years, these minutes flying around. In the middle, the eye of the hurricane. That moment, that moment is all there is: always. Because tomorrow is today, and yesterday is tomorrow. There are no differences, no rewinds, no fast forwards. It is here. It is right now. We can't count on the promise of tomorrow, the distance song of coming years. Because tomorrow, because the coming years are here, are right now, are this very moment. Change doesn't happen overnight, but if it happens, it surely happens today.

Day 67

"Pay attention to what you receive.

What you already have.

It's true that what you focus on expands.

Life is a reflection of who you are.

So increase, develop you.

Be more and life will reflect that."

Zen Mirrors

DAY 68

ALARM BELL

We all know that your addictive feelings of course won't go away forever when you decide to quit for good. Instead of fighting against it, use your addictive feelings as an alarm bell. Because they do serve a purpose, namely: there is something wrong. When you start recognizing this, your addictive cravings could serve you enormously. Instead of giving in to the craving, you could simply ask the question, *'What is there I need to hide from in my life right now?'* And deal with the answer in a different way, not with the destructive solutions of your addiction.

DAY 69

Situations, people, news events that trigger certain emotions are a great source for gathering 'data' about your unconscious. Especially when your emotional response is disproportional to what actually is happening. For example heavy anxiety for talking to a stranger. Think about that for a second: is there a great physical danger for talking to a stranger: in almost all cases, no. So why the fear? Today do an inventory of what situations, or what people, or news events, or social media posts, etc, trigger a disproportionate emotional response within you. Shine the light and unravel your unconscious.

DAY 70

What lies did you tell yourself to continue your addictive behavior?

Day 71

A SPIRAL

If you want to know your future, discover your patterns. Life is like a spiral. Follow the line of addiction and you will end up, eventually, in total destruction. The intention of addiction is to numb the pain, and then to numb, and to numb even more. To drag you down. It's a spiral that leads to utter and final destruction, the destruction of you. Unless you make the conscious effort to align to a new spiral. Repetitive thoughts lead to repetitive actions, leads to repetitive results. That's why for a lot of people life doesn't seem to change all that much. Some faces, workplaces, outer appearances change, but the overall state of being, and thus experiences, won't change all that much.

Day 72

"When you imagine something,
Life has opened the road to a new reality,
And life will show you the tools you need,
If you decide to follow that road."

Zen Mirrors

DAY 73

GRATITUDE

It's easy to forget. Certainly amidst every day's troubles, certainly amidst the struggles of recovery. But it's important to hold still for a while. To realize the gift of life. To breathe it in. To look around. To feel it. That spirit of life, of flow, of love. This doesn't mean to be positive all the time. It means to pay attention. To things, people, experiences. We tend to take them for granted so easily.

Paying attention and being grateful could turn all these ordinary and dull moments into something a bit more extraordinary.

DAY 74

"What a miracle to take the burden of someone's chest.
To lay the hand of forgiveness on someone's cheek.
Saying, it's okay, it's all okay.
Dissolves the pain of weeks, months, years, in seconds."

Zen Mirrors

Day 75

DETERMINATION

Imagine you are in a pit, darkness surrounds you, but there are just enough resources to keep you alive. By realizing that there should be more to life than thick darkness, you start to climb. And climb. Until one morning you are seeing a light, a hopeful, beautiful light. But then, because your power is weakened by the effort of climbing, and disbelief you fall down. You are back on the ground, surrounded by darkness again. It might seem you are back to point zero, with even less power than before, but that's temporary. And it isn't the truth. You've seen the light. Now you are at point zero, with a knowing there is light shining above. Realizing within that addiction is a reality, a spiral you no longer want to descend in is a vital step. That knowing is the light. When you have seen it, when you have felt the determination to break the cycle of addiction, that determination will always be available to you.

Day 76

"Seeing is not believing
- it is only seeing."

George MacDonald

DAY 77

What does it tell you about yourself that still, after the horrors of addiction, you've found the courage to choose for recovery?

Day 78

Enough Is Enough

You decide when enough is enough. And now is as good as time as any to decide so. Break the agreement that you have with addiction from the core. When you decide that you've hit rock bottom, you are saying to yourself: I no longer identify myself as an addict. Or I no longer let addiction take control of my life. That's the declaration that from now on forward you are aligning with recovery. Then, when a relapse does occur, after you've decided enough is enough, it's a part of your recovery. It's no longer another victory of your addictive self.

It's a stepping stone towards the greater freedom of lasting recovery.

Day 79

"We are living with an ever-present arrogance that tomorrow will come. And next year, and someday. But we all have a deadly illness called Life on Earth. Waiting becomes an illusion. What is there within you, to be done, to be said, to be felt.

Go then, and do, and say, and feel. Be, here, now."

Zen Mirrors

Day 80

The Light Of Awareness

If you are starting to become aware of your state (addiction), and what the contents of these states are (beliefs, thoughts, sensations, actions), that state will lose its powers. Destruction starts to evaporate in the light of awareness. If you don't pay attention, years can go by where nothing seems to change. Decades even. But the moment you start observing, everything changes. And then, reality becomes malleable. When you are beginning to grasp the enormous meaning of these words, the infinite sparkle of change will ignite within you. Addiction, very soon, becomes a tiny dot in the landscape of possibilities. You will step over it swiftly, and, on your way to the new, think to yourself: *Well, what else is possible?*

Day 81

"It is easy to tell the toiler
How best he can carry his pack
But no one can rate a burden's weight
Until it has been on his back"

Ella Wheeler Wilcox

DAY 82

DISSOLVE THE CHAINS

Here and now you can make that choice, to break the bond with addiction. To declare yourself independent from it. Dissolve the chains. Quit the agreement. It will call, shout at you. And maybe, yes, you will come back to it. Maybe again, and again. But each time it will be with fresher eyes. Cleaned by the spirit of awareness. You will see addiction crumble. Detect it's lies, it's secrecy, it's dirt & tricks, and it's utter, utter smallness.

Until the dark monster becomes nothing more than a tiny dot.

DAY 83

"The most powerful form of prayer, and the one which can virtually gain all things and which is the worthiest work of all, is that which flows from a free mind. The freer the mind is, the more powerful and worthy, the more useful, praiseworthy and perfect the prayer and the work become. A free mind can achieve all things."

Meister Eckhart

DAY 84

If your addiction was a person, how would you describe him or her?

Day 85

During the road of recovery, you discover lots of new insights. Sometimes this is frightening, because it means you have to reevaluate your old beliefs. It could mean that you were not right. And actually, to me, that was one of the most fascinating parts of my recovery journey. The discovery of a new thought, a new belief. It helped me to grow. Grow away from my past. Put a healthy distance between me and these low vibration thoughts and sensations. Traveling new roads leads to new discoveries. Be open to it. If you want or have to change your life, new beliefs are mandatory.

Day 86

Personally, I have accepted the addiction as a part of who I am.

I talk to this part of myself every now and then and make sure that it won't sit on the throne of my kingdom again. But it can be, like any other part of my personality, a great advisor. Now, I see my addiction as a friend. Because of the loud voice of addiction, I always know exactly when something is wrong in my life. I thank my addiction for speaking up and then I decide to solve the problem in a constructive manner.

Day 87

HABITS

"Habits are powerful, but delicate. They can emerge outside our consciousness, or can be deliberately designed. They often occur without our permission, but can be reshaped by fiddling with their parts. They shape our lives far more than we realize—they are so strong, in fact, that they cause our brains to cling to them at the exclusion of all else, including common sense."

Charles Duhigg, *The Power Of Habit*

Day 88

Working on yourself can be overwhelming. Taking action on your goals, working on your health, finances, social life, all of that: it demands your time and energy. But that's not it. You have your work and other every day obligations. A vital part is finding harmony in once life. Relaxation is one of the keys to balance out work and effort. Try to take a moment for yourself every day, or share a moment with your loved ones, where you just are in the *here* and *now*. Enjoy these moments, hours, days. Why not give relaxation as much importance as effort. Try to find how harmony works for you.. Resting isn't without value; it's the time you take, to refresh.

Day 89

Dissolve The Chains

Addiction is a direction with one, certain direction. There is a choice we have. In the grander scheme of things. To descend or to ascend. Every moment we can make decisions that shape our destiny. Shape our reality. Addiction drags you down, lower and lower. Again, and again, repeating the same cycle. With more pain. With more numbing. It's only when we are within that storm, that it may seem it will last forever. That there is no way out. That the craving forever will persist. And that you just, can't say no. I just can't control it. But the storm is a phase. It's a moment you're stuck in. It's your Groundhog Day. A vinyl that's on repeat. And after hundreds of times, the music is fading, and noise starts making its way in. How to stop the noise? Escape Groundhog Day? Find your way out of the storm?

It is to realize that this too is malleable.

Day 90

Write down all the fears you feel when it comes to a relapse. Making the unconscious, conscious. And make that what is rushing through your mind, concrete. Awareness will help you to deal with fear, and it will diminish the fear.

DAY 91

Who would you like to be one year from now?

Day 92

Liberate The Old With Awareness

Awareness is the key. The key to a better life. Always. It liberates the old. To welcome the new, push forward with your dreams, your desires, your vision of a life that differs, that is in glory. Liberate the old with your awareness. With the exercises and information in this book, with all else you find helpful, with guidance from a Higher Power, and guidance from your Higher-self. With your incredible inner strength, with the knowledge that love conquers all. And welcome the new by aligning to a reality you prefer. By determining what kind of life you would love to live.

Even if that vision is merely a life of peace and stability.

Day 93

"Let nothing perturb you, nothing frighten you.
All things pass.
God does not change.
Patience achieves everything."

Saint Teresa of Avila

Day 94

Don't Be Alone

When you've made the decision for recovery, don't be alone. You could share your decision with the friend, family, professional worker or group you've contacted to talk about your addiction. Asking for help doesn't make you weak; it is the only smart way to know your weaknesses and give yourself the extra power of another person or support group to fight something as big as an addiction. Define for yourself how you want to be helped. For example, the option of calling someone when you're having a really hard time with your addictive thoughts, having an accountability buddy, or simply ask the other person/support group what they suggest. For most addicts, it is one bridge too far to really seek professional help, and yes, there are other ways to do it. But it's going to be hard to do it all on your own. So at least share your story and find the courage to ask for help in whatever way suits you best.

Day 95

"Happiness is like a butterfly which, when pursued, is always beyond our grasp, but, if you will sit down quietly, may alight upon you."

Nathaniel Hawthorne

Day 96

The word spiritual is not about letting go of your material possessions, or relationships, or career. In the literal sense of the word. But the road of spirituality will help you to deal better with all that is right in front of you. To stop being someone you're not. To embrace the true you.

If anything it will make it easier to manifest what you truly desire. But without the attachment to things or titles. Just with a genuine love for you, for others, for life: and from that state of well-being, the journey of life not only becomes easier, but it will also be experienced more fully and with more enjoyment.

Day 97

"If you are distressed by anything external, the pain is not due to the thing itself, but to your estimate of it; and this you have the power to revoke at any moment."

Marcus Aurelius

DAY 98

If today you had all the courage in the world, what three actions would you take?

DAY 99

THERE SHOULD BE MORE

The final stages of my gambling story. Unfortunately, that wasn't the last time I gambled, but it was one of my last episodes. I've lost tens of thousands of Euros over my seven years of gambling. I lost an insane number of hours aimlessly watching live sporting streams in the middle of the night, tired and irritated while losing over and over again. There were points where continuing to smile seemed to be an option no more. Times where I couldn't see the near future. But somehow, whenever I woke up the next day I always had a feeling that this couldn't be what life was all about. That this wasn't the purpose. That there should be more. Much, much more. No, people are not meant to be on this earth just to fight an addiction.

DAY 100

When you feel strong enough, it is time to take responsibility for the problems that you've caused with your addiction. It's best to first take care of yourself. Like in any emergency, make sure you yourself are safe. Then it's time to deal with the consequences. I strongly advise you not to wait too long with this. It hurts to confront yourself with the consequences of your addiction, with all the pain you have caused yourself and others, but don't walk away from this suffering.

DAY 101

INSPIRATION

Your life is in constant motion. Goals and new habits, could quickly fade away due to every day tensions. When you're unaware for a prolonged period of time, you can get sucked into a life you don't want. One way to dodge this bullet is to stay inspired. This can be done through daily journaling, proper relaxation, and giving your mind a healthy diet of inspirational content, conversations and thoughts. Because inspiration, most of the time, isn't given to you; you have to seek it. And even if it is just there: you have to allow it to land.

DAY 102

Instead of playing out their craving, they resist it. With great force. A children's hand trying to hold the wild ocean from overflowing the land. And on the surface, it may go all well. But when the source of the craving isn't met. Isn't faced. The craving will return. May not in drinking, but then in playing cards. May not in playing cards, but then in drinking. Or softer equivalents.

What must change is the source. And the source is you.

DAY 103

MAN'S SEARCH FOR MEANING

I am moved and inspired by Viktor Frankl, a psychiatrist who survived Auschwitz in World War II. He wrote a well-known book entitled *Man's Search For Meaning* about his experiences at the concentration camp, which he survived.

I want to share an excerpt from his book here:

"The way in which a man accepts his fate and all the suffering it entails, the way in which he takes up his cross, gives him ample opportunity—even under the most difficult circumstances—to add a deeper meaning to his life."

DAY 104

"No man, for any considerable period, can wear one face to himself and another to the multitude, without finally getting bewildered as to which may be the true."

Nathaniel Hawthorne

DAY 105

Write down five positive associations you have with recovery.

Day 106

A Purpose

When addiction is present, life is contracted. No freedom can be invited because the house of your being is way too small. For most, the next step is recovery. And while it is better to be in this stage than chained as an addict, preoccupation with recovery can soon become a very small house too. In this house, you will live with the forever fear that the scary guest will return. Afraid for the next glass, dice, or the lurk of heroin.

But what can become of an addict? Is the only phase she will experience next, to be the one of a recovering addict?

To me, this much is clear: nobody has come to this earth, solely to fight an addiction.

Day 107

"One ought, every day at least, to hear a little song, read a good poem, see a fine picture, and, if it were possible, to speak a few reasonable words."

Johann Wolfgang von Goethe

DAY 108

TRANSCEND ADDICTION

"Mindfulness is not just a state of passive acceptance, it is a way to actively pay attention. To your life goals, the people around you, the world around you. Furthermore, it helps to examine your worries and anxieties. Just paying attention to these negative thoughts is sometimes enough, to let them disappear. And at the very least mindfulness will give you a stronger stand whenever negative thoughts are trying to take control of your life."

21 Exercises

DAY 109

I invite you to let you guide yourself by that version of you that is sick of addiction. That is sick of the repetitive cycle of recovery intentions, followed by relapses. By that part of you that intuitively knows that there is a way out of this rat race of madness.

Read on, because there is a level of being where you simply can't longer attract addiction into your life. Where you move away from addiction. Not with forceful recovery, where you have to fight every day for the rest of your life, but a state of being where addiction simply dissolves.

DAY 110

PACE

"Quiet minds cannot be perplexed or frightened but go on in fortune or misfortune at their own private pace, like a clock during a thunderstorm."

Robert Louis Stevenson

DAY 111

I speak to your belief in a life beyond addiction, and beyond recovery. Everything happens at the right moment, there are no coincidences in this universe. Wake up to the fact that addiction, just like anything else, is just a matter of you attracting what you are. And what that means eventually, is that change, big change, beyond the limits of recovery is awaiting you.

Certain energy attracts certain realities. Be in a higher state of energy and everything changes, your perception of the past, your perception of the now, your chances for the future. It is a circle that transcends time.

DAY 112

WEEKLY REFLECTION

Write down one or two experiences from the past that had a life-changing effect on how you see yourself.

Day 113

Instantaneous Pleasure

Every bad habit and every addiction serves a purpose. It grants you instantaneous pleasure. You can attain it without much effort. It won't take any effort to grab a fourth beer on Tuesday night, eat your third piece of apple pie in the middle of the night, or play that video game. (Only in the last stages of a destroying addiction does it become difficult to continue the habit, due to either a lack of money, the possibility that others might find out, or because you've made it difficult for yourself to continue. For example, not being in control of your own money anymore).

Day 114

"Before my definite decision to stop drinking, I've had times of sobriety. It never lasted. What was positive though, during those short periods of sobriety, I learned new coping mechanisms for the times when I usually drank. New hobbies, positive self-talk, accountability, and healthy self-care all became useful weapons in my battle against alcohol. The game changer for lasting recovery is both a practical plan to overcome your unhealthy drinking habit and a full understanding of why you are continuously pouring these glasses of alcohol." - Joanne Edmund, *Quit Drinking*

Day 115

If the first thing you do in the morning is checking your phone, scrolling through Social Media and checking the news you might have some different thoughts than yesterday. A shooting in a high school in Virginia, bombs in the Middle East, an old college classmate showing his new B&W on Instagram and your uncle sharing a picture with his new girlfriend on Facebook, adding a text: *Never too old to learn.* You're up-to-date on that news now...

A morning ritual is meant to get you ready for the day. Both everyday thoughts, most of them limiting, and mindlessly scrolling through social media and news sites won't get you there. It will suck you into the fires of the Middle East and party photos of friends and hold you there for the rest of the day.

Day 116

"By three methods we may learn wisdom: First, by reflection, which is noblest; Second, by imitation, which is easiest; and third by experience, which is the bitterest."

Confucius

Day 117

Power Questions

Start your day in a conscious, quiet state. No phone, no news. This is the start of a new day. A new day in your life. Give yourself the time, energy and focus you deserve. Don't let the rest of the world suck you into its negativity (aka the 'news') or into their lives, however good it may seem (social media). So, then what?

Ask questions. Power questions. It will change your focus immediately. When you're out of bed and preparing your breakfast you could ask yourself, for example,

What am I grateful for in my life?

What in my life am I proud of?

What am I excited about today?

Day 118

"There are only two ways to live your life.

One is as though nothing is a miracle.

The other is as though everything is a miracle."

Albert Einstein

DAY 119

WEEKLY REFLECTION

Why are your qualities much needed during these times? Write down at least three reasons.

DAY 120

WORTH EVERY STRUGGLE

Just quitting your addiction is one thing. It is what you get back when you quit or no longer overindulge in something that you feel true joy. Besides the incredible change in my financial situation, health, productivity, and social life, the change I am most excited about is the change in my consciousness.

Finally, I feel strong, secure, and self-confident enough to experience life fully. I'm no longer in my head all the time, which allows me to finally connect with the people I love so much, as well as new people. I can enjoy the fruits of life with integrity, as I can respond to any personal problems in a strong and constructive manner. This feeling of control, of enjoying life and most importantly, of truly connecting with other people, is worth every struggle that the gambling addiction brought to my life.

DAY 121

"Resolve to be thyself;
and know, that he who finds himself, loses his misery."

Matthew Arnold

DAY 122

GOAL SETTING

The importance of goal setting was proved in a famous study among Harvard MBA students. Of the entire class, prior to graduation 84% of the students didn't have any goals at all. A minor 13% of the class had set written goals but had no concrete plans. Only 3% of the class had both written goals and plans to achieve these goals.

The results were stunning. In a follow up of this study done ten years later, it turned out that the 13% of students with written goals earned twice as much than their fellow students who hadn't set any goal. That's not everything. The 3% with both written goals and a plan did far exceed the rest of the class. They made ten (!) times as much as the other 97%.

DAY 123

"Far better it is to dare mighty things, to win glorious triumphs, even though checkered by failure, than to take rank with those poor spirits who neither enjoy much nor suffer much, because they live in the gray twilight that knows neither victory nor defeat."

Theodore Roosevelt

Day 124

If you want to reveal what kind of feelings you are trying to hide by your addiction, recovery is a procedure that could take months. And for some much, much longer. But even in a shorter period of time, you can take giant steps to proactively deal with the consequences of your addiction, building up the inner strength to combat your addictive cravings.

Most importantly you can find meaning in your life by working on your talents, connecting with others, and enjoying life to the fullest.

Day 125

Keeping a journal is the more conscious way of keeping a diary. Instead of just writing about your experiences, you reflect on them. And you reflect on your thoughts, your goals, your flaws, your strengths, and so on. It's a daily practice to strengthen your mind and find new strategies to achieve or change your goals.

Over time these series of journals become a helpful go-to guide to study your progress and setbacks in life, and learn valuable lessons for the future.

DAY 126

Describe your Inner Critic.

What would be an appropriate name for him or her?

DAY 127

NOT BOUND TO ANY HABIT

I hope you will find the wisdom to transcend the craving.

Cause you're not bound to any habit.

Not even a persisting and destructive one.

But also, there should be no chain to recovery.

For neither addiction nor recovery is a prison for life.

My writings, my work is dedicated to that greater truth.

DAY 128

A path to break through the suffocating walls of addiction. A way out of this endless seeming fight with addiction. I write for you, who knows that her life, his purpose here on earth, is bigger than giving in to the craving, or struggling for recovery. That addiction is just a phase of life. And so is recovery. These words are written for those of you who believe in these statements, or who have the hope that these statements are true. Because I do believe that you can be freed from the chains of addiction for good. Not just living life as a recovering addict, but to live a life as you.

As who you are meant to be.

Day 129

Life After Addiction, Life After Recovery

We have to find the you that is inviting the addiction. The you that is resisting it. And then transcend from there. Cause there are levels of being where that storm no longer can rage. Levels of being high above the craving. From there addiction is but a distant memory. You won't look at it with anger, nor with regret. But with compassion and mild interest. And you will be grateful for the lesson its claws have scratched upon you.

Yes, I want to shout it out: there is not only life after addiction. There is life after recovery too.

Day 130

A book is merely a book.
Words are merely words.
In and of themselves, they bear no magic.
But you, within yourself, have the power to transform words.
Into hope. Into better thoughts. Into better actions.

And eventually, into change.

DAY 131

AN EXCITING FUTURE

In times of boredom, procrastination or when you're about to give up, the purpose behind your goals (the why) can help you to get through. One of my goals was to live for three months in South America. The thoughts, images surrounding that dream, made it quite easy for me to do the work that would allow me to make that jump.

It's about excitement. That fuels your work ethos. It colors your life. What are you excited about? What is your motivation to get out of bed? Make it a part of your goals. Create an exciting future for yourself that you would like to walk into every day.

DAY 132

"If a man does not keep pace with his companions,
perhaps it is because he hears a different drummer.
Let him step to the music which he hears,
however measured or far away. "

Henry David Thoreau

DAY 133

What is the role of most mass media in shaping our beliefs for this world? Is it a message of love or one of fear they share?
Reflect on that answer.

DAY 134

LOVE FOR LIFE

At a certain level of being you will no longer attract addiction into your life. You are no longer occupied with recovery. You are no longer living ashamed of the past. You are no longer in continuous worry about the future. You're simply be, simply live, simply do what you came here for. Fulfill your mission here, whatever that is. To become a cook, to study history, to raise a family, to make a movie, to be a teacher. Know that what inspired you to seek a way out of this harsh circle of addiction, is something higher up the scale than the addiction itself. That within you are already levels that surpass the craving, surpass the shame, surpass frustration. Those are levels of courage, of compassion, of intellect, of joy, of peace, of love. Levels that motivate you, uplift you after another addictive rage. After another relapse. After another streak of bad news. It is the light within you, it is what corresponds with the highest form of power in this universe, that soothes, heals, and dissolves the darkness. It is the love for life, the love for yourself that brought you here.

DAY 135

"It is love alone that gives worth to all things."
St. Teresa of Avila

DAY 136

MEDITATION

Your thoughts hold an enormous power on your overall well-being. Left unexamined, they decide your destiny in life. When you can control your mind, anything is possible. Controlling thoughts, however, requires work. Sit still for one minute and pay attention to your rushing thoughts. They go anywhere, demanding you to go with them. Even if they go to places of anger, frustration, craving, worry or sadness. The best way to regain control over your thoughts is through meditation.

Meditation is the art of paying attention, increasing your awareness, and letting go. On Day 104 you were given a short meditation exercise. Hopefully, you've already made it part of your daily or weekly routine. It can make a significant difference in your long time happiness and success, but it will also give you an immediate feeling of calmness and joy. A double reward.

DAY 137

"The world as we have created it is a process of our thinking.
It cannot be changed without changing our thinking."
Albert Einstein

DAY 138

WAKING UP

He doesn't need to play the roulette. He needs to find the doing, that enlights his spirit. Nor does she crave the bottle. She merely seeks to *be*. One moment. One lifetime.

Craving is the lesser alternative for one who isn't yet. Hasn't become. It can take a thousand spins, a thousand bottles to understand. To accept the calling. Of your soul. Of the universe. Speaking. Louder and louder. Through the spins. Through the bottles. Saying, wake up. To wake up. To wake up.

DAY 139

In Leo Tolstoy's acclaimed novel The Death of Ivan Illich one of the main characters is contemplating the following question on his deathbed: *"What if my whole life has been wrong?"*

Why do we wait to live the life we're meant to be? To fulfill our calling. The present doesn't have to be a continuation of the past. There is the beauty of a new beginning, every day, each moment. Don't wait on your deathbed, it isn't worth the risk.

Day 140

Draw a graph representing your life over the last 6 months.

DAY 141

A GLIMPSE OF HOPE

A glimpse of hope in a pile of dust. Deep down you know you can choose. You know you can open the door to a new life. That belief, that inevitable fact, gives you the direction to control your problems. To cure your addiction and find out what it really is you're trying to numb. Choose the right way.

This moment always has the life-changing opportunity to change. To choose a different decision that leads to a new life.

DAY 142

The most important thing is to be that version of you who is no longer addicted. Anything you will ever do in a recovery process is about that: to align with a version of you who is not addicted.

You can find that version of you already within.
He or she is already here.

So make that your primary task: to discover the you who is no longer addicted and to align with him or her.

DAY 143

DO YOU SEE WHAT I SEE?

"But to be angry at myself or at my addiction isn't the right way.
Understanding my addictive behavior has given me peace.

It wasn't the drinking that was the core problem,
it was the pain that I needed to numb."

Joanne Edmund

DAY 144

In every moment there are a trillion choices we can make. Countless
parallel universes that may exist. What do we choose? Or maybe even
more important, who is in charge? Why do we keep making choices
knowing it brings us suffering? Then what is life but a series of
uncontrolled repetitions...

Is it?

Do you see what I see?

Is reality fixed?

DAY 145

CONNECTION

We tend to be most grateful for the moments we share with other people. Friends, family, acquaintances, colleagues, even strangers. When you truly connect with someone else, there is this sparkle of magic. It does good to take care of these connections. By paying attention when you are interacting. To see the other as a whole human being. To be present. To listen. And to speak authentically.

Also, try to take care about your existing relationships. Don't take them for granted. Take care of them, as you would take care of a lovely garden. Is it time to have that much needed heart-to-heart talk with your loved one? Or do you still need to thank a good friend? Reunite with an old acquaintance?

DAY 146

Small steps have the incredible power to become big changes. Both destructive and constructive (positive). I frequently ask myself

"What is one thing I can do today to make this day worthwhile?"

It's a simple question, but the benefits are hard to exaggerate.

DAY 147

How can you create a healthy balance between solitude and socializing?

DAY 148

AN ACTOR

We put a mask on our face. And through this mask, we see life in a specific way. The mask: *I am a receptionist, or I am a doctor. We change our roles, often, I am a daughter, I am a father, I am the one who needs to bring harmony, I am the rebel, I am the addict, I am the hero, I am the victim.*

You are an actor, with multiple roles per day. And you go on stage every day. The important thing to understand about addiction is that it's like a role. With your addiction comes a certain script, thoughts, beliefs, a story you tell yourself. Certain emotions and sensations. Certain places and objects. Even a certain look and facial expression.

And it's an incredibly heavy role to play.

DAY 149

"The best portion of a good man's life: his little, nameless unremembered acts of kindness and love."

William Wordsworth

Day 150

Making A Shift

In a way, saying *I am an addict* is inaccurate. More accurate would be, you're playing out addictive behavior. You have the whole range of levels of consciousness to your disposal, and you've simply tuned in to addiction. Your being has aligned with the pattern *Craving* → *Relief* → *Pleasure* → *Suffering* → *Craving*, so that's playing out in your life. Over and over again. Within you, however, are the means to tune into all kinds of channels. If you're in a state of anger, or courage, or productivity, or love: there would be a whole other reality you experience. But, saying I am an addict is simple and at least it shows that you're owning your addiction, instead of running away from it. By not running away from it and taking the steps towards overcoming it, you already declare that there's a new story within you that is waiting for its turn when addiction is shown the door. Don't be discouraged by the past. Don't be discouraged by relapses. Life can change very, very quickly when you make a shift within.

Day 151

"Let us be grateful to the people who make us happy;
they are the charming gardeners who make our souls blossom."
Marcel Proust

DAY 152

LONELINESS

When I look back on my addiction years, one of the saddest memories is the overall loneliness I felt. The secrets, the lies, the shame that led to these moments of solitary existence. Of isolation. During my recovery journey, I made it my first commitment to heal the bond with myself. To find a way to finally accept myself. Because of my financial situation, I wasn't able to go out much during my recovery. During the many nights sitting alone in my apartment and working on myself, I always felt a whispering sense of loneliness. Although I knew I was on the right track, the one thing missing was connection. Looking out the window and seeing a young couple kissing, holding hands…

I felt like an outsider. Not just to the young couple, but to the rest of the world. I was constantly listening to Fast Car, hearing Tracy Chapman singing, *And your arm felt nice wrapped 'round my shoulder*

I had a feeling that I belonged I didn't belong. Or, so I thought. But then it dawned on me, why should people come to me? And actually, they did come to me. Asking me to go out. To join them. But I was too afraid to admit that I didn't have the money to go out. I was digging my own grave.

That night I decided to not just make the commitment to create a better bond with myself, but to create a better bond with others as well. To give what I sought. And to accept, receive when it was shared with me.

I firmly believe that life is not meant to live alone. I believe that you project to others the relationship you have with yourself. So my lack of self-acceptance at that time made me feel uncomfortable to be with people. With or without having the money to join them.

It was like a mirror.

When I started to reach out, I realized once again how lucky I was with my friends and family. And how warm and intriguing it is to meet new people and feel this magic sparkle of connection.

DAY 153

"If you've come this far on your road to recovery, it's easy to overestimate yourself. What harm will it do to go to a bar, if I know I'll only drink a beer? What harm will it do to meet my old drinking buddy again? What harm will it do to forget my new, constructive habits for a couple of days in a row? What harm will it do if I have just one drink... Throughout your recovery, remember this one sentence: *The best friend to relapse is overconfidence.*" - Joanne Edmund

DAY 154

WEEKLY REFLECTION

Write down the three biggest lessons you have learned from your addiction.

Day 155

Small Steps

A lot of people who are into self-development are falling into the trap of wanting too much in a short amount of time. This willingness is where get-rich-quick gurus build a fortune on. However, lasting change doesn't happen overnight. It's an in-depth self-discovery journey combined with taking consistent small steps that lead to the big changes. It will take time, however. And that's okay. The journey itself is where you can focus on. Where, between hard lessons and moments of conflicts, you find joy & confidence about your silent progression.

Day 156

Definitely, there is no magic towards the first stage of recovery: you just have to quit. But there is life after that initial stage of fighting. After the relapses. There is a whole land of possibilities that awaits you, once you've shrugged off the role of 'being' an addict. This book is not written with the intention to become a fighter against your addiction for the rest of your life. It's written to help you to overcome it for good, and to revive your hopes and dreams. To help you realize that life isn't over. That the past shouldn't dictate the future. And that you have it in you to make a fresh new start.

DAY 157

MONEY

Money is a vulnerable topic to talk about. For a lot of people, money has some sort of association with evilness. I personally believe that the lack of money is the root of all evil. From top to bottom it's greed for money that does no good. The good lies in between.

Money is neutral. You can do great things with money, like building a hospital. You can do destructive things with money: like bombing the hospital. It is an energy mover. Establishing a healthy relationship with money is what you should seek. An income that suits your monthly expenses, a steady and ever-growing savings account and/or investment account & an accurate monthly plan to pay off your debts. Paying attention to your finances and making it grow (reaping and sowing) is a fine and stable foundation for living the life you want to live. Don't let the lack of money ruin your life. And start aligning to the abundance that's already all around you.

DAY 158

"I'm not strange, weird, off, nor crazy, my reality is just different from yours." - Lewis Carroll

DAY 159

PART OF RECOVERY

You will start noticing that when you move away from addiction, that different thoughts will arrive.

And after an initial period of changing thoughts, your words will reflect these thoughts.

Eventually actions follow as well.

DAY 160

Relapses do happen. For almost all of us, it's part of recovery.

And it is not the end of the world.

What matters is how you deal with it. It is simply a signal that you still have work to do on your recovery journey. Maybe you have to tweak your approach here and there. First and foremost you have to think about how you deal with it, when a relapse occurs. Preparation is gold. You will thank yourself for it later.

DAY 161

Write down three things you could do to recover from a relapse.

Day 162

The 'Right Now'

It is hard to exaggerate what could happen once you know you're on the right path. It takes action, uncomfortable conversations, rigorous self-reflection and awareness. But glimpses of light make it all worth. Because it is not about the future. It's never about the future. It is happening now.

You can make the right choice each moment. Literally every moment. Because this moment, the 'right now' is all that we have.

When you do what is right, the moment changes.

Your life changes.

Day 163

Being aware, or living in a state of mindfulness, is a continuous state. It is a choice to shine the light on 'everything'. Your own life, suppressed emotions, thoughts, your mind and the world around you.

It is a freeing state of living, where you face your fears and give yourself the opportunity to truly live the life you want to live.

DAY 164

A NEW ROLE

By deconstructing your addiction, you will gain a full understanding of how it works. About all the dirty tricks it plays. This knowledge, this awareness not only greatly diminishes the chance for a new relapse, it also diminishes the fear for relapses. And it will help you with understanding why you're choosing for addiction and how to deal with it in another, positive way.

Awareness will help you to break the agreement you have with playing the role. By breaking that agreement, by stopping to identify yourself as an addict, everything becomes a part of the road to recovery. A new role will slowly emerge: a new reality will slowly emerge.

DAY 165

"Do not spoil what you have by desiring what you have not; remember that what you now have was once among the things you only hoped for."

Epicurus

DAY 166

AN OCEAN OF KNOWLEDGE

It's amazing how many lessons you've actually learned in your life. How many times you've picked yourself up. The values of these lessons are often not seen.

Try to look at your past as an ocean of knowledge, waiting to be used.

DAY 167

Yes, there is more to life than addiction, and there is also more to life than fighting an addiction. You being here, on this planet, is reason enough to believe that you too are here with a purpose.

Addiction has come into your life for reasons, maybe not yet known to you. But there are lessons to learn from it. Maybe you can't see it yet, but it will come to you when the time is right.

Nothing happens by accident.

Now it's time to move on and start your next phase.

Day 168

Weekly Reflection

Write down the best ways to recharge your batteries.

Day 169

Giving

There is a magic power in giving. Wholeheartedly giving, without expecting something in return. During my gambling years and the first period of my recovery I had periods where I had an intense feeling of loneliness. An endless black pit. One day I decided, instead of waiting in my apartment with the curtains closed, to give what I wanted myself: connection, inspiration, love.

Eventually it came back tenfold.

Day 170

Everyone has a specific purpose here on earth. In your craving, you are learning lessons at this stage of life. It's an experience you need to go through, for reasons often unknown to us. But it is just a stage. The next stage is awaiting you. Life, the Universe, your soul they're rooting you on to learn the lessons of this stage. Eventually, life is not a game of comparison. But it is about the experience. You need to go through different stages to find the real you. Who you've always been underneath the stories, the thoughts, the labels, the limitations. To let go of all of this and reach the highest, finding the divinity within.

Day 171

Worth Each And Every Step

"No matter how bad life seems in this moment, it is never too late to start over. Nobody is destined to be miserable and tied indefinitely to an addiction. With time and effort even the worst situation becomes manageable, and over time will seem like a distant memory. Your addiction is not your purpose, every human being is destined for so much more. First of all, to enjoy life, at least a tiny bit more. I won't lie, this will be a difficult road, especially at first. You will need help and support to move along this road. Facing the unpleasant shadows of your past. But soon, you will also realize that this journey is worth each and every step." - Joanne Edmund

Day 172

The time, energy and thinking someone wastes on addictive behaviour; what if one uses that for something else?

Can it be that on some level an addict develops his or her creativity enormously because of the elaborate ways one uses to continue the addiction? And if that's right, what are the amazing creative possibilities for one who "conquers" his or hers addiction?

DAY 173

MASTER OF HABITS

This is an interesting story about a gambling addict who also replaced his addiction, right after he decided to quit. He told me that for the first week after he quit, he felt so tired that he decided to take a one hour nap each day, right after work. Two hours later he went to play tennis with his best friend, who knew his gambling secret. He told me that the very act of scheduling in his nap didn't make him feel guilty, because he knew he needed it. By scheduling it in for a specific time period, he was the master of this little habit of napping. That feeling of mastery, even if for a seemingly silly but necessary activity like taking a nap, was (so he told me a couple of months later) what gave him the confidence to believe that if he could master one action, he could master another. And another. And his addiction.

DAY 174

"It's really a wonder that I haven't dropped all my ideals, because they seem so absurd and impossible to carry out. Yet I keep them, because in spite of everything, I still believe that people are really good at heart."

Anne Frank

DAY 175

If you'd meet your addiction today, what would you like to say to it?

DAY 176

GIVING

The question I got some time from people, is,

"Are you never afraid your addiction will return?"

And it is a fair question. A thought that is in the back of the mind of most recovered addicts. First, I believe you have to stop identifying yourself as *'an addict'* or *'a recovered addict'*. For the purpose of clarity, we're using *'recovered addict'* to advertise my books. But in reality I don't identify myself as a *'recovered addict'*, but just as a person. As me. And as 'me' there are a thousand things that can happen. I have influence on the course of my life, but far less than I like to believe. I am not afraid that my addiction will return. I know that my intention is right and life will always give me exactly what I need.

And winters are a normal part of life.

DAY 177

"Attention is the rarest and purest form of generosity."

Simone Weil

DAY 178

RELEASING

There is a collective fear for not being good enough, for abandonment (rejection) and for uncertainty. And we have ingrained these fears even heavier through our childhood experiences. We all have our traumas, the truly severe, and the one that on the surface doesn't look so bad. But to the impressionable mind of an up growing child rejection, being left alone, criticism, uncertainty can imprint heavy insecurities for life.

That is if we do not consciously dive into these 'traumas' and release them.

DAY 179

"As human beings, we can choose how to react to addiction and recovery. I believe it doesn't matter whether you have been an alcoholic for a year or for your entire life. You always have the opportunity to change at this very moment. In every moment.

Your response can change your life."

Joanne Edmund, from *Quit Drinking*

Day 180

Fading Away

When I no longer saw myself as an addict, nor as a recovered addict, the thoughts of addiction, or you could say the level of craving, was gone. Or was it the other way around? It doesn't matter too much.

When you are no longer aligning yourself with a particular story, that reality will fade away. And that can happen in a fantastic, almost magical turn of events. It can happen fast, extremely fast. When addiction was out of my life, it was not all joy and roses.. But the life I was living, was considerably better, as you can understand, than the life of an addict.

Day 181

Relax properly.

A great source for relapses is feeling of stress. It's about not taking good care of yourself. Bring habits into your life that will help you with self-care, such as taking multiple showers, or a bath per day, taking a nap, getting a weekly massage, going for a relaxing walk, playing a board game with friends, encouraging self-talk, journaling and so on.The options are limitless.

DAY 182

What message would you like to share with the rest of the world?

DAY 183

A COMPELLING DAY

Motivation and goal setting goes hand in hand. When you feel ready and motivated, the question remains: 'What are you going to do today?' That's where goal setting comes in. It doesn't have to be elaborate, or an extensive to-do-list. Rather not. Set one or two main goals for the day, and one or two minor goals. That's it. What's most important is that those goals will drive you to rock your day. Not just words on paper, but the creation of a compelling day.

DAY 184

Addiction is a cycle that repeats itself over and over again. And it becomes heavier and heavier. It's how life teaches us. The first lesson is mild. And the longer we don't grasp its teachings, the harder the lessons will be.

You can stop that cycle by learning the lesson. Transcending it. Finishing that part of your education and moving on. Letting go of the energy of addiction: the low vibrational energy of craving. Your beliefs will change. The addiction loses its heaviness, it's power. Slowly but surely the addictive thoughts will disappear.

DAY 185

RELEASING

Something I never thought possible before happened in the course of a few weeks, my urge to gamble dissolved almost entirely.

Before this shift I had intended to stop gambling, with the usual, *I never gamble again* after a big loss. Of course, that never came to be. But after this shift in belief, adopting *Gambling equals losing money* I only had one more relapse, about six months later. And it was not a 'rock bottom relapse' either, it was one small bet. Although I had more money deposited, I withdrew that money that was left and I never gambled again. Also the fear for gambling, for a gigantic relapse that would wipe away all my savings, resided. More slowly, to be honest, but it disappeared until the years of gambling became a light memory. A lesson from the past. Gambling became something that I saw as recreational. Something I just wasn't interested in.

DAY 186

"What lies behind us and what lies before us
are tiny matters compared to what lies within us."

Ralph Waldo Emerson

DAY 187

STOP GAMBLING

I didn't go to Gamblers Anonymous, nor to a therapist. Even in the days of darkness I always had this glimmering hope that light would come in again. A feeling of optimism that has been with me throughout my life. I guess that drawing big circles around the problem, spending years to come to the 'source', was not where I was looking for. Where I was looking for was astonishingly simple: *to stop gambling.* And being recovered, I discovered that healing the source was profoundly more easy when you came from a place of stability.

DAY 188

There will be days that all the work you've put in and all your good intentions may seem useless. Times when it will be difficult to sit down and do what you know you have to do. Hours where you want to close the curtains and lock the door. Minutes where you feel down, fearfully, and stressed. Moments where the will to act courageously, to act from the heart, is threatened by devilish temptations. You are going to make mistakes and different problems will arise. There will be fresh tears and unhappy moments. Lasting recovery won't change that. But it gives a new perspective and hope in the beginning, and it gives purpose and energy later on.

DAY 189

What is your body trying to tell you in the last few months?

Day 190

A Great Powerful Step Forward

In a way recovery is simple: just stop drinking, stop gambling, stop eating junk food, stop watching porn, stop taking drugs. Or control it at least. Simple, but not easy. The key question is: how to get there. How to create this shift in identity. To change the one who faces the mirror. To let the belief *Drinking is toxic and it ruins my chances to take care of my children*, win from the sensation, *I need to drink to feel relieved.* Sure sometimes there are medical and/or heavy psychological issues at play. And in any case I think seeking professional help with recovery from addiction can be a great step towards faster and lasting recovery (a necessary step in life-threatening cases).

But if you still feel the power within you to work on yourself, to become aware of your problems: deconstructing your addiction and replacing toxic thoughts with thoughts of hope, light, energy, and love is a great, powerful step forward.

Day 191

"Look beneath the surface;
let not the several quality of a thing nor its worth escape thee."
Marcus Aurelius

DAY 192

A STRONG RESILIENT AND CARING PERSON

Recovery gives you the strength, the deep inner strength, to deal with the storms and rain in confidence. As a strong, resilient and caring person. You will feel peace of mind, courage, and an undeniable feeling of self-confidence and a love for life.

DAY 193

"Everyone with a drinking problem is resourceful to find ways to deceive and kid themselves into thinking that one or two drinks will not be a problem. As long as it is within reason...

There will be times when the urge seems insurmountable. All your good-hearted intentions are now seemingly overthrown by the craving for alcohol. Rather than giving up, it's in these moments you realize that this craving is the very problem. And recovery, with all its might and strength, is exactly your choice because, in time, it will overthrow the dependence for alcohol. When you reconnect with yourself and your life again, a bigger purpose will slowly emerge. A goal, a vision, a future far away from intoxication. It will shine light over the shadows of your addiction."

Joanne Edmund

DAY 194

NOW IT WAS MY TURN

There is a time in every person's life when he or she realizes it's time for a change. That time where your life can make a turn for the better. That all-deciding moment.

I was already into self-development and practiced a lot of positive self-talk. I held the powerful conviction that I was worth more than being a prisoner of self-destructive behavior, addiction, and limiting beliefs. Millions of people had led the way for me. Inspiring stories of people who take back control of their lives and find success are not hard to find nowadays.

Now it was my turn.

DAY 195

"Psychologists distinguish a benign habit from a harmful addiction when the primary reason for continuing the behavior is no longer to gain good feelings, but, rather, to avoid the negative feelings associated with stopping the behavior or withdrawing from the habit."

Harriet B. Braiker, Ph. D, *The Disease to Please*

DAY 196

When was the last time you overcame failure? Write down one or two lessons you have learned from that.

Day 197

Repeating Patterns

Some situations in life seem to happen over and over again. Yes, there are new people, a slightly different income, maybe even a new environment, but the core of the situation keeps returning. Always giving more in a relationship than the other, always going up and down in weight, or never truly expressing yourself at your job. Time may continue linear, but what about you? Are you really progressing? Or are you just running around in circles?

You are in a relationship, or finally found your dream job, or you are 'working' on yourself heavily: but in what ways are you just repeating your childhood? Or your teenage years? Where in life are you repeating patterns over and over again?

What lessons do you need to learn in order to really move on...

Day 198

"To be what we are,
and to become what we are capable of becoming,
is the only end of life."
Robert Louis Stevenson

DAY 199

MANIFESTATION

Nothing you have manifested in your life is there without your agreement. Even the things you don't like. What you can change instantly is how you attend to these agreements. How you respond to a break-up, financial loss, problems with your health. Or how you respond to success, to the gifts you are receiving every day of your life, to your personal growth. That's the incredible power you already have: the way you respond. And to what you respond.

Very soon, your outer life will reflect your new inner life.

Manifestation, when you let go of all the luggage you have collected throughout life, becomes easier and easier.

DAY 200

"Do not be anxious about tomorrow,
for tomorrow will be anxious for itself.
Let the day's own trouble be sufficient for the day. "

Jesus Christ

Day 201

The Light

Make a commitment to yourself to never turn off the light on in your own life ever again. The best way to do this is through positive self-talk, journaling, or a mindful state of awareness.

When you keep the light on in your life, you are addressing your problems and desires in a conscious way, so that they can't sneak off and hide in dark places in our unconsciousness. Keep practicing self-talk, journaling, or a mindful state of awareness in a warm, considerate, friendly, and inspiring way.

Day 202

Today, let's take a look at the manifestations in your life you don't like. Write down at least three situations in your life you worry about, or you're frustrated about. Especially ones that keep coming into your life over and over again.

Then write down why some part within you secretly like these things to be manifested over and over again. What is the secret pay-off?

Again awareness will help change your life in truly astonishing ways.

Day 203

A drawing, short story, or poem that portrays your authentic self.

DAY 204

YOUR HEART

We are so washed up in our thoughts, that we become more and more disconnected from the gift of intuition. Your heart is an extremely, extremely intelligent place that can lead the way for you.

It has answers.
It is a place of peace and trust.

Focus on your heart area when you want to know answers. And let your mind help you with the practical matters. For most people, this is far from the reality they live in. They rather trust the mind, or other people, or news outlets' opinions on what to do. But it is all limited, all destined to keep you in the same circle of yesterday. Of the past.

DAY 205

"The intuitive mind is a sacred gift and the rational mind is a faithful servant. We have created a society that honors the servant and has forgotten the gift."

Albert Einstein

Day 206

Unveil The Truth

It's time now, you are ready to unveil the truth within and the external truth. You are ready to follow the call from your intuition, the knowledge that you have deep within about your true purpose. About how you can serve. About what you would truly like to experience now, and during your lifetime here on earth. With connecting to your heart, to your intuition, Higher Self, you are connecting to the Source. The Universe, God, or how you would like to name it.

Day 207

"The desire to drink may always be present. In time it will not be all-consuming, but the desire may pop up unexpectedly. Those are exactly the times you must explore why the desire has resurfaced. It usually means you are in a situation you wish to escape, or you feel bored, or need to numb your feelings. Instead of reactivating old, destructive habits use what you have learned so far, and with awareness, patience, and strength, guide yourself from the craving for alcohol to the solution of the real problem. This way, you could use the 'addiction cue', as a reminder that something in your life needs attention." - Joanne Edmund

DAY 208

HEART CENTER

For today, try to make connection with your heart center. Your intuition, your Higher Self.

What answers, directions are awaiting you?

First, write down two or three questions you would like to be answered. Then go down in deep meditation and ask these questions to your Higher Self. Keep your awareness on your chest area. You can place your hands on your heart, to help to make this awareness more potent. We recommend a meditation of at least ten to twenty minutes. You can do this with music or a guided meditation. Meditations can be easily found on YouTube. Search for: Higher Self Meditation, Heart Meditation, Soul Meditation, etc.

After the meditation, write down the insights you have gained.

DAY 209

"Doubt everything.
Find your own light."
Buddha

DAY 210

How would you describe yourself?

DAY 211

PURSUE YOUR DREAMS

"Did you find where you were looking for?

Pursue your dreams or stay where you are. In the end, is there a difference? You get to decide.

If you went to the doctor for a routine check-up and, horrifically, the doctor said you were going to die, not in a year, not in six months, not in a week, but that very same night, how would you look back at your life? What would people say about you? What was your contribution to this planet and humanity? Your family, your close friends, your life. What did you make of it?

Most likely, you're not going to die tonight. So the answers to all these questions are not definite yet. You have time. What will you do with it?" - 21 Exercises

DAY 212

"If you look the right way,
you can see that the whole world is a garden."
Frances Hodgson Burnett

DAY 213

UNVEIL THE TRUTH

Sad thoughts, limiting beliefs, procrastination, and tough situations: they don't simply go away when you decide to quit gambling. Setbacks and feeling unhappy sometimes; these are part of life.

Yet we're always in control in choosing how to react and handle these situations and feelings. One of the best ways to stay on the right track is to look for inspiration. Fortunately, we live in an era when there's an abundance of helpful information.

Unquestionably, you will have to focus on making peace with your gambling addiction, but as discussed earlier, you are more than your addiction. Inspirational/ self-help (audio) books and videos, self-help groups and forums, self-help programs and personal coaching can all really help you take your life to the next level.

DAY 214

"How wonderful it is that nobody need wait a single moment before starting to improve the world."

Anne Frank

DAY 215

FEAR

"To feel fear is normal. To succeed in life and to achieve your goals, you must act despite fear. It's very difficult to get rid of fear altogether and that isn't the goal of this exercise. The goal is, rather, to be aware of fear. Once you identify it, you can consciously decide whether you let fear control your actions and behavior.

Remember, you are not your fear.

It's just the mind talking. With consciousness, you can support your own desired decisions. It may take a while before you've mastered this and that is fine. Just take small steps to go in the right direction."

21 Exercises

DAY 216

"Human minds are more full of mysteries than any written book and more changeable than the cloud shapes in the air."

Louisa May Alcott

DAY 217

Write down three empowering things you can do to deal better with worries.

Day 218

What Would The World Do Without You?

"Examine your potential. Discover strength.

Creativity is the key to solutions.
The door that leads to answers.
Nurture it.

What would the world do without you?

So many souls that'd want to be touched...
So many people are waiting.
The world needs a fresh breeze of authenticity.
Of you, doing what you need to.
However small it may be.
The world needs you. Your love. Your talents. Your everything.

Don't wait no longer, The time is now.
It's up to you." - 21 Exercises

Day 219

"Peace is always beautiful." - Walt Whitman

Day 220

Hear The Perfect Song

Little boy, lost in the woods. I hear the perfect song, far, far away. Stop the wandering. In woods of thoughts. There, in darkness, craving is your King. How far are we gone? In sticky thoughts, sticky like syrup, where are we free? To choose. Breathe my boy, breathe. And stop. Stop for one moment.

Look around. Smell. Listen.
Hear the whisper of trees.
See the dancing of plants.

Then the thoughts, the syrup, as through a magic wand, will disappear. Gone in thin air. For all that is a lie will crumble in sight of truth. And truth is touched upon in silence. In holding still. We need no more than one moment to crush the lies. To hear the perfect song.

Day 221

"Don't let a day go by without asking who you are...
each time you let a new ingredient to enter your awareness."
Deepak Chopra

DAY 222

SURRENDER

Don't make your recovery the obsession of fighting these sorrows.

For then addiction and recovery goes hand in hand. Then, they're two sides of the same coin. Climbing one or two steps. With the fear of going back these steps in a heartbeat. One disappointment away from these times of rain. The times of storm.

Choose recovery not of fighting. Choose one of surrendering. It is in letting go the universe works best. In letting go that you can climb unencumbered. Soon you see that as addiction, recovery is just a phase. A next phase already awaiting you. To help you climb onwards: hear then of the levels of being.

DAY 223

"If you eventually accept a lost opportunity of the past a substantial psychological burden will be lifted. Don't let your mind trick you into thinking your life is over because you lost one opportunity. It's just not true. Find peace with your past and tap into your inner wisdom to find new ideas and answers that will lead you to new opportunities." - 21 Exercises

DAY 224

WEEKLY REFLECTION

When did you feel truly abandoned? And what can you say to that version of you who felt abandoned?

DAY 225

WHAT WOULD THE WORLD DO WITHOUT YOU?

Certain energies attract certain realities.

Like attracts like.

As the clean streets in a good neighborhood, and the dirty streets in a bad neighbourhood. Not a question of what comes first, but a continuous cycle. Where everything is connected. No first, no second. No second, no first.

So tell me then, to what man, to what women is the reality of addiction attracted?

For it was said, that what you think you become.

And the wiser man knows that you attract what you become.

DAY 226

"You are where you are in life because of what you believe is possible for yourself."

Oprah Winfrey

Day 227

Lower & Higher Levels

Does it mean that by simply aligning to a level of productivity your addiction will disappear?

In a way yes.

If you are busy creating a website, you are not engaging in addictive behavior. But, of course, it isn't that simple. Because addiction has been imprinted so heavily in your current belief system, it will creep back in over and over again. Addiction has become your habitual level of consciousness. In order to get out of it, you should seek to engage yourself in higher levels habitually, until a new level of consciousness overrides the old. You need to learn the lesson of how to stay away from addiction for good, to move up indefinitely. In this book, there are plenty of tips on how to do that. But as stated earlier, awareness is the beginning. You need to become aware of what keeps you in these lower levels.

Day 228

"It is never too late to be what you might have been."
George Eliot

Day 229

Into The Woods

You can't hold back the water. The storm. The rage. Restriction leads to destruction. Open up. Your voice, your pain, your anger. Addiction is a form of self-expression. A very destructive one. It won't stop until you listen. You can numb it for years, even in recovery. Even when going to meetings. Even when reading a recovery book. Even when keeping a journal. Sticking feathers up your butt doesn't make you a chicken. Listen to the pain. Really listen.

Go into the woods.
Go into the darkest place of the wood.
There are no monsters under the bed.
Find the source.

Day 230

It's time to stop regretting the past. Enjoying the *now* is your most important 'task' in life. There is nothing more in life, than right here and right now, as the book *The Way of the Peaceful Warrior* by Dan Millman teaches. Having a compelling dream can definitely help you to better enjoy life. Doing so will allow you to try, take action, fail, learn, and grow.

DAY 231

WEEKLY REFLECTION

A drawing, short story or poem portraying something small, almost insignificant, that is beautiful.

Day 232

Dance, Go, Live

Life's too short to wander around in the dark,
Regret all the things you've done wrong,
Or think about how life could have been.

Go out in the world,

Enjoy the company of close friends and family,
Start your own company,
Record your first song,
Teach your son how to fish,

Dance, go, live.

Day 233

While one paradigm is not better than another,
They can all be appropriate for different purposes,
It goes without saying that the paradigm at which you are
Will determine how much you determine life as struggle.

DAY 234

ESCAPING THE JUNGLE

"Escaping the jungle of shameful and drunken nights. Of lying and deceit. Of lost hope and gruesome regret. Standing tall on a new day. Making the commitment one day to never drink again. Relapses come and go, but what stays is the knowledge and a growing confidence that you will never surrender to your old choices. Accepting the power of your addiction but not giving in. Rising to the occasion, to face the struggle, face the fears, the painful insecurities, again and again, until you find the truth. The root. Then and there, your addiction wavers and you realize your power. Over it. Over everything inside of you. You see the new horizon, a glowing light, more beautiful than anything you've ever seen before. In the mirror you see a person with fresh eyes, self-confident and smiling, and before long you will realize the weeks, the months, the years of fighting were all worth it. You realize the mighty, beautiful person looking back at you in the mirror, is you." - Joanne Edmund

DAY 235

"Imagination does not become great until human beings, given the courage and the strength, use it to create."

Maria Montessori

DAY 236

SURRENDER

As any author who writes about self-development, or anyone who has invested a lot of time and energy in both self and spiritual development, the topics of self-responsibility and a "positive" outlook towards life are hard to deal with. Because one always feels the need to somewhat defend him or herself for the belief in self-responsibility, and for the belief that what you sow you reap, both positive and negative. They go somewhat against the beliefs of the majority of the people still have, that leans towards, *life happens to you*. On a next paradigm starts the belief that you are the creator of your own life. Yet at one higher paradigm, it is seen that the field, the universe is the source of your life. This by no means gives up your power of choice, but it will make you a bit more humble on the one hand and the other hand you recognize that if you collaborate with that field, with the universe, extraordinary things are easily possible.

DAY 237

"If you tell the truth, you don't have to remember anything."

Mark Twain

DAY 238

WEEKLY REFLECTION

What problems in your life could actually be opportunities?

DAY 239

BELIEFS

If you believe only the rich can get richer, you can only be rich if you already have money. If you believe you can only be rich, if you take a lot of action, you can only be rich when you work your ass off. If you believe you can be rich, just because you are, you can be rich whenever you feel that is an appropriate reality to experience.

For all beliefs, however, effort is needed to go from one place to another.

Again, the difference will be experienced in how that effort is perceived and how much effort is required.

DAY 240

Isn't that the purpose of life on earth, to discover, to learn, to grow? Is it not the nervousness before that first date, the process of falling in love, discovering your childlike self in his or her presence, the most fun instead of 'having' a relationship? Is not the effort of starting a side business, discovering the entrepreneur within you and creating a product the most fun instead of 'having' an x-amount of money directly?

Day 241

Slow It Down

If you truly choose a reality that fits you, the beliefs, thoughts and actions should fit you like a king's mantle. Sure some of the actions are new to you, challenge your comfort zone, but the discovery of these actions, of how it works, will be much, much more enjoyable than the force you need for holding together a life you don't want. Or for the action required for creating a reality that is good for gaining approval but is not truly authentic to you.

So try, here and now, to make a commitment with yourself to lay off all these layers of yourself that were determined by your environment. The gaining approval madness that circles through your head.

Slow it down. Slow it down. Slow it down.

Day 242

"When I let go of what I am,
I become what I might be."

Lao Tzu

DAY 243

One day for yourself. Where you are just with you. Do some reflection on your life up till now. *What is life trying to tell you?* What are things that repeat over and over in your life, that is not to your liking? When was the last time you laughed so much it hurt? When was the last time you sang? You danced? What are some of the dreams you still have? What makes you feel self-confident in your life right now? What doesn't?

Ask some of these reflective questions.

Take a break. You don't have to swim upstream all day, let alone all week, or all month, or years, or even decades. Relax and reflect. Buy your favorite soda, or go out into nature, or to your favorite park, or just lie in bed. Connect with the one who is experiencing this life in the past, in the future, right now: you. If you think you can take a break of a day, then do it for half a day, or for two hours, or just one hour. Don't rush through this book, looking for the next solution. The best results with any book, any guru, workshop, or method will be there when you've already found some of the answers within. Then the book, the guru, the method will only add to that and can speed up favorable experiences a bit more.

DAY 244

What are things that repeat over and over in your life, that is not to your liking?

DAY 245

What makes you feel self-confident in your life right now?
What doesn't?

Day 246

Dance, Go, Live

It could be a good exercise every once a while, to just sit down and write down all of the positive options you have for the coming hour, the coming hours. Be a bit creative, try out some new things, give more attention to old things.

Life doesn't have to be boring.
It is rich. Rich in options.

Even when negative things occur, there are many different options to react to these adverse events. Don't get stuck in just doing the things the old ways. Examine life. Be an adventurer in your choices.

Day 247

It is tough to take a good look at your own life, certainly when life is clouded by addiction. In self-reflection, however, lies the astounding power to lasting change.

How could we change ourselves,
if we don't know what is beneath the surface?

Day 248

Escaping The Jungle

It is not about traveling, bungee jumping, and discovering the secrets of the pyramids. An adventure can be discovered close to home. By giving some real attention to your loved ones, to your job, your hobbies, and discovering new things. This open attitude will help you with creating a new reality.

And you are already a person that knows that there is more to life.

That there is always a choice, always a turn for the better. So when reading this book, take on the attitude of the adventurer. The man or woman who is confident enough to discover. With that attitude, it will be much more likely that you can truly familiarize yourself with your new chosen reality. And if you know, embody it, that reality will be much more likely to manifest as a fact.

Day 249

"What a grand thing, to be loved!
What a grander thing still, to love!"

Victor Hugo

DAY 250

CREATING A NEW HABIT

The best way to create a new habit is picking a specific time each day. It could be a part of your morning ritual, or during your lunch pause, or at the beginning of the evening. Pick a time that feels right to you. Want to have a backup? Then pick a second time each day where you could do this new habit if somehow the first time won't work. Don't beat yourself up if you forget, or for some other reason didn't do it one day. Even if it is out of procrastination. Don't even beat yourself up if you didn't do it for two days, or three days. This negative approach will only drive away from the new habit further. Be kind to yourself. Simply ask yourself why you feel the need to keep procrastinating? Maybe this new habit is at this moment not yet important to you, or it is too much. Discern between genuine reasons, and reasons from the ego to resist effort. You know yourself best. Effort is required in life, but force is something else. That said, sometimes is effort in the face of setbacks or procrastination a magical solution to fast, positive results.

DAY 251

"To reach something good, it is useful to have gone astray."
St. Teresa of Avila

DAY 252

What two or three people are triggering you the most? Why?

Day 253

I Give Back The Rhythm

To experience something better, effort is required. Set the train in motion. Your feet in unknown land.

The most magical effort there is in life is effort that is repeated over time. The training of an athlete, the daily writing of an author, the daily loving attention of a mother for her child, it is like life says:

"You put in the effort, I give back the rhythm"

Positive effort in that way will be returned by a beautiful song.

Day 254

"We share this planet. We share the same insecurities and the same dreams. Above it all, we share our love and the need to connect with each other. Without sharing, there is but cold indifference. To share, we need both to receive and to give. You give money to a charity. You receive a nice compliment. Good, loving energy needs to flow from one to another. Be open and be willing to give and receive. Someone who receives love honestly and thankfully will be significantly more likely to give love in return." - 21 Exercises

Day 255

Escaping The Jungle

Major changes start at the foundation.

Timewise, only taking actions corresponds with the slowest form of growth. This is contrary to the belief of the masses that action moves mountains. Better is it to first change your thoughts, before taking actions. Because your actions will be much more fruitful. And change will be much more rapid.

Even better is it to change certain beliefs.

This will change all the underlying thoughts, and therefore the actions you take. The most rapid change happens when you change the being, because changing your core belief, will change the underlying beliefs, and therefore the thoughts, and therefore the actions.

Day 256

"When you arise in the morning think of what a privilege it is to be alive, to think, to enjoy, to love ..."
Marcus Aurelius

Day 257

Change

A person desperately seeking for a partner, with the paradigm '*action moves mountains*', goes through hours of relationship videos, many more hours of worries and thoughts about how to find the attractive partner. There will be many dates, many flirtations, many online conversations. He certainly finds dates, maybe even many dates. Most certainly he could find a partner, maybe even many partners. But all of it will be surrounded by struggle. By force. It is a state where your attention is narrowed. Focused on the persistent action of getting what you want. The higher you go up, from first changing your thoughts, to changing your beliefs about relationships, to changing your core beliefs of seeking approval; the less struggle is necessary to find your perfect partner. The action that is taken from that state, will feel more natural. Here you understand that if you come from the belief of chasing, chasing is where you end up with. Transcend the chasing, by being authentic. *Being you.* And opportunities for relationships arise all around you, blossomed like roses, abundant like sunshine.

Day 258

"A thing of beauty is a joy forever." - John Keats

DAY 259

Everything you see around you was once thought.

What does this tell you about the mind?

DAY 260

Thoughts Are Limitations

Almost all thoughts we have are limitations.

They're necessary for us to understand life. To stay in a safe bubble from which we can grasp the incredible, unlimited size of everything. But they are, what they are: just thoughts. And they come from mere beliefs. Created or adopted by ourselves. There is frankly no limit to how much you can possibly earn. But for most people, a net monthly salary of 50.000 USD is crazy money. This amount of money is peanuts for a world-renowned soccer player, while his salary is nothing compared to the billions of Jeff Bezos. And the billions of Jeff Bezos are nothing more than the tiniest piece of water molecule in the infinite ocean of abundance of the universe. To realize this, to acknowledge your own limiting beliefs can be a major step forward. Because this can mean epic creation. Beyond your wildest dreams.

DAY 261

"Alcoholism took away my pride, my ability to love, and my ability to feel. Recovery has brought all of it back. The mighty waves of addiction weren't enough to drown me. The water has become calm and steady again." - Joanne Edmund

DAY 262

ESCAPING THE JUNGLE

Back to the *wildest dreams* of Day 260.

For most people *life beyond your wildest dreams* isn't at all necessary. Just going on a nice date, feeling a bit more healthy, finding a new exciting job or publishing your first book, is more than enough. For now.

Take a moment and contemplate your own dreams. Maybe not yet your far-away dreams of a house by the lake, of raising a family, of making a Hollywood movie. But your plans, your desires for the near future.

What are they compared to that vast ocean of abundance?

DAY 263

"Whatever is rejected from the self,
appears in the world as an event."

Carl Gustav Jung

DAY 264

THOUGHT-PROVOKING QUESTIONS

Let's ask some thought-provoking questions today. To use our imagination for rapid change. For inspiration. Think about what you would like to achieve in your life within three years. Then ask yourself the question, How could I achieve this in one year? And how can I achieve this in six months? And how can I achieve this in three months?

The next thing you do is think about the masters in your field of choice. For example if you think about improving your overall fitness, you write down your favorite sportstar, or if you want to improve your calmness in life, you write down your favorite guru. Then ask the question how would he or she achieve this goal within six months? Within three months? Or within 40 days?

This exercise can help you to come up with new ideas. *Outside The Box* ideas indeed.

DAY 265

"Your task is not to seek for love, but merely to seek and find all the barriers within yourself that you have built against it." - Rumi

DAY 266

What three (small) new and exciting things can you experience in the coming month(s)?

DAY 267

How To Succeed In Life?

One needs to grasp at least at a basic level the concept of self-responsibility and needs to have incorporated a good portion of optimism within him or herself. It is the person that knows that if she wants things to change, she needs to do it herself, that will be much more likely to succeed, then he who waits in apathy for the circumstances to change. And it is he who doesn't wine too long over a setback that will be much more likely to succeed than she who drowns herself in self-pity and drama after the first storm.

So check it with yourself, where are you on that level of self-improvement? Big soul searching isn't needed at this point, but if you feel you lack self-responsibility, it is good to toughen up a little. And if you feel setbacks have the better over you the majority of the time, it is good to relax a bit more and develop a more positive attitude towards life.

DAY 268

"Care about what other people think
and you will always be their prisoner." - Lao Tzu

Day 269

Compassion

Send compassion to a charity, a cause, people, or a lonely part within yourself. You can do this through voluntary work, a charitable gift, sending a prayer to a cause, or to people close to you that encounter hardship, or to contact a lonely part within and just be there with yourself. And to be understanding.

The act of compassion is an infinitely good thing you can do to help humanity improve their general state of being. Or some might call it, to raise the energy level of yourself and thereby the energy level of humankind.

The giving of compassion is a two-way street. By doing it, not only the receiver receives love, but you, as the giver will feel that love twofold when you send it.

Day 270

"Your visions will become clear only when you can look into your own heart. Who looks outside, dreams; who looks inside, awakes."

C.G. Jung

DAY 271

WHAT ARE THOUGHTS EXACTLY?

This exercise is not about what kind of thoughts you have. It is not an exercise for the intellect, but for the observer. Almost all of our problems in life come from our thoughts. You think you have to be rich, you think you have to escape, you think she will never like you. But what we forget in 99% of the cases, is to look at what it actually is the cause of so much pain. For at least ten minutes sit down and observe your thoughts. To help you to come in this observer state, start with three deep breathing cycles (breathing in, breathing out). Then, just observe whatever thoughts come up. About the groceries you still have to do, about a person in your life you love, about the meaning of this very exercise, etc. But instead of determining the meaning of these thoughts, observe what these thoughts actually are. Are they words, or sounds, or images? Where do they come from? Where are they located? And where are they going? It is good to gain some perspective on that which creates so much suffering. I recommend doing this exercise at least three times on different days, to gain a more clear perspective of what your thoughts are.

DAY 272

"Stop thinking, and end your problems." - Lao Tzu

DAY 273

What simple pleasures did you enjoy this week?

DAY 274

SEEDS

The tremendous power of thoughts come from the fact that they are the seed of our actions. And therefore they might seem like the seed of our destiny. Learning about states of consciousness, you start to understand that the different levels attract different kinds of *seeds*.

What is important for now, is to see is that our thoughts are not random seeds. But they are seeds attracted to the field, the state of consciousness we are in. This means that to change our destiny, it is not really about the seeds, it is about our state of consciousness.

It is not about what we think or do.
It is who we are, that matters.

DAY 275

Addiction shines through some of our worst thoughts, some of our worst emotions, and consequently bad actions. Destructive actions. Do we see the sunset, the almost purple looking sky? Do we perceive our greatest talents, our ability to create, to make intelligent choices, to love? It is extremely limiting what addiction has to offer. It is the running gag of a madman.

DAY 276

THE MIRACLE OF LIFE

The miracle of life is not in some destined future.

It is already here. Already within. Feeling good is the state of being we are all looking for. All of your wishes are just a way to get in touch with that feeling. If you can find that feeling in the here and now, simply, without going through years of struggle to first achieve financial independence, or to first find the perfect partner or to first achieve the ideal weight, then that is an enormous power. Because from that *feeling good* not only will what you set out to do be more effortless, you might also discover that the things your desire in life are not the actual things you want. This state of feeling good can then be the starting point of either effortless actions or effortless new discoveries

DAY 277

Where there is low, there is high.

There can't be one without the other.

Find that place above the craving.

And then go higher.

From a safe place you can reach the you who is below.

Day 278

Dissolving The Spider

The attachment to escapism is within all of us. Frightened for our shadow self, frightened for the pain, the tears of the past, we seek distraction. And the more unaware, or the more scared you are to face these inner demons, the stronger the attachment is created. The stronger the grip of the spider. And the worse of you are.

But the spider can be dissolved.

Realize that facing these inner demons might be frightening at first, but the more you come to know them, the less scary they become.

Day 279

Just start today. You don't always need an exact plan.
Creativity, success flows with effort.

So if you would like to write a book, start writing a couple of hundred words today. Anything. If you want to become a salsa dancer? Start dancing today. Even if you have to do it alone. Practice in front of the mirror. Don't have a mirror? Practice without the mirror.

DAY 280

Why is your life a true miracle?

Day 281

Rock Bottom

The turning point doesn't have to be sleeping under a bridge, stealing your children's money, prostituting yourself, or seriously jeopardizing your health. It's often when you decide enough is finally enough and then you go one step lower. And sometimes another. And another.

The pull of quitting needs to be bigger than to pull to continue. Simple physics. Again that pull doesn't have to be as dramatic as if you don't quit, you can't see your children anymore or if you don't quit now, you seriously might end up in jail. It can be as 'small' as if you don't quit now, you waste more time than you can otherwise be spending on writing a book, finishing a study, or starting a business.

Hitting rock bottom is a decision you make yourself.

Day 282

Stare into the shadows of the future and see yourself smiling, celebrating a remarkable achievement… What a skill do we possess as human beings. Being able to set goals. Being able to create the future at any time in our life. Today you are creating yours, in all consciousness.

Day 283

Little Boy's Song

The shadow breaking my soul
And nowhere to find a single world glow
No star bright enough for pleasing the night
Waiting were all
To hear little boys' song in smiling delight

And thus I returned
For singing a song
Finding out then
That nothing was gone

Day 284

"Every heart sings a song, incomplete,
until another heart whispers back.
Those who wish to sing always find a song.
At the touch of a lover, everyone becomes a poet."

Plato

Day 285

Dissolving The Spider

We are all caught by our thoughts.
They are rushing.

One moment you worry about your relationship, the next you think about grocery shopping. A web of thoughts spinning around us.
It occupies our attention from moment to moment.

Day to day. Year in, year out.

There are glimpses of consciousness in between.
Moments of awareness where you suddenly escape the grips.
A moment of life.

Day 286

"In the end,
The treasure of life is missed by those who hold on
And gained by those who let go. "

Lao Tzu

DAY 287

Fast forward, ten years from now. You are meeting your ten-year-older self, what kind of advice would she or he give you?

Day 288

Before you go to sleep, you can shortly reflect on your day.

What lessons did you learn that day?
What made you proud of yourself?
And what are things to be grateful for?

It is a time to take a step back. To become aware of you actually did that day and what it means to you. A life worth living is a life worth recording.

Day 289

"We are living with an ever present arrogance that tomorrow will come.

And next year, and someday.

But we all have a deadly illness called Life.

What do you wish to do before you die?

This becomes a very potent question.

What is there within you, to be done, to be said, to be felt.

Go then, and look for it." - Zen Mirrors

DAY 290

DESIRED REALITY

Describe in detail what you would like to attract into your life. Keep it simple. Take one area of your life you want to improve. For example better health, a better dating life, improved finances, and so on. Tip: lie down for about ten to thirty minutes with your favorite music. See the details of your desired life. Let it come up. Afterwards write it down. Describe how your life is currently in the area you want to improve. Think about the actions you take in that area, the repeated thoughts you have, the repeated results you sow, your facial expression, the people you compare yourself with when it comes to this area, and so on. Now look at the two realities: your old one and the desired one. Describe the fundamental differences between the two. And see what you can do to come closer to your desired reality.

DAY 291

Stop giving in to the craving. Stop resisting the craving. Transcend addiction. Transcend recovery. For there is a bigger you awaiting: the problems of today will soon be seen small and insignificant tomorrow. It's not magic I am teaching. It's a bit more knowledge about life. About what attracts what. And, most importantly, to crush the "truths" that you can never be free again.

DAY 292

PLAY & EXPERIENCE

You don't need to wait to experience the reality you desire. Start experiencing (part of it) it now. Write down all the objects that come with your desired reality. For example, if you want to create a part time business, objects could be: a notebook specifically for business, a whiteboard to write down your ideas, etc. After you've finished the list, make the commitment to yourself to buy at least one of these items within the next seven days. And start using it.

The most common excuse when it comes to self-improvement is: *I don't have the money to...* Let's agree that you don't fall into this category. One of the few perks of a lack of money, is that you need to be creative in order to arrive at a certain solution.

DAY 293

When you take this amazing opportunity to make something of your life you will soon find out that your addiction past is something that belongs there: in the past. You are so much more than your addiction! Breathe, smile and be grateful. Take small steps, don't be too hard on yourself and make your life count!

Day 294

If you had only one more year to live, what would you love to create?

DAY 295

CONFRONTING YOUR FEARS

By daily confronting your fears, you will send a strong message to yourself:

I am no longer letting my life be controlled by small, negative thinking.

There is an incredible force that will be released once you put your thoughts on paper. Negative thoughts go literally out of your head. And once on paper you will not only better understand them, but also make better decisions once such a negative thought tries to control your life.

DAY 296

Things will be okay.

Don't be discouraged.

You will know what to do when the time comes.

Don't escape to the past of the future. Be here.

That's the lesson now. That's the next stage.

Be here. Be, be, be. That's all.

Let go.

Take that jump in the present moment and else will follow.

DAY 297

INTERRUPT THE FRANTIC THINKING

Try to observe your thoughts from time to time.

Interrupt the frantic thinking.

Catch them before they go into the full pattern.

DAY 298

You can only shift when you become aware.

That, awareness, it's a superpower. Available to all of us. The time has come to use this power for the good. For the right things. For releasing the chains. For breaking through the walls. Get to know your addiction. Dive into it. Don't let it escape no longer. Demand it's attention.

Who is he? Who is she? What does it want? What tactics does it use? When is it active? What lies does he tell? What secrets does she keep? Deconstruct it.

Until the beast is no beast anymore.

But just a pattern of thoughts, sensations, activities.

Day 299

Love To Discover

"Humans are go-getters. We love to discover. And in that discovery, we can find our happiness, every step of the way. If you start questioning yourself, question reality, you soon start to see the infinite possibilities that you're surrounded with. That reality is a reflection of who you are. And the alignment to the reality you prefer is already within. What holds us back in most cases are thoughts, beliefs, of how things should be. This journal will help you to make that fundamental shift from impossible to possible. To free the way for a life of authentic self-expression, abundance, peacefulness, and the ability to cope with problems that will inevitably still meet you on this journey."

21 Exercises

Day 300

The noise, the storm they are vibrations of energy. As long as you agree to addiction, it will be present in your life. It's within you. It's your being that aligns with that dense reality of craving. And it is within your being where there is a way out. The attention needs to be shifted. Upwards. To the light. To joy. To peace. To freedom. To a deeper, more awakened experience of life.

DAY 301

WEEKLY REFLECTION

Write down a compelling list (12 or more) of all the things you're grateful for in your life right now.

DAY 302

AWARENESS IS THE FIRST STEP TO AWAKENING

We live inside our own reality.

Our own belief systems, our own stories. Awakening means seeing life, seeing reality as to how it really is. If you want to know what your beliefs are, what your stories are, look around. What does your reality look like?

Awareness is the first step to awakening. And with that awareness, you can slowly, but surely let go of these stories that don't serve you.

DAY 303

Three fears that almost all people are run by, are: The *fear for abandonment* (I am different, that's why attracting a partner is so difficult for me, fear for rejection, etc.), The *fear of not being good enough* (I can only express myself, if I am perfect, Only when I am in a relationship, I feel worthy, etc.) and The *fear for uncertainty* (Only when I make this amount of money, etc.).

How do these fears show up in your life?

DAY 304

REWRITING A BELIEF

Your life is most likely a repetition of certain patterns. Things will only change for real when you let go of these patterns. Why do you need to add, to chase, to be more, to have that relationship, that amount of money, that amount of freedom? You will be surprised how worthy, free, light, united you feel when you let go of the burden of these stories. These labels. These words of fear.

Meditation can greatly help you in this process. Especially when you're doing it daily. Today we're going to rewrite your stories. Pick a story, a fear, a belief that doesn't serve you. y Then rewrite that story into a statement that truly serves you. You can do a meditation first, or take a moment of silence to ask your Higher Self, or The Universe to help you during this process.

DAY 305

"Mistakes are, after all, the foundations of truth, and if a man does not know what a thing is, it is at least an increase in knowledge if he knows what it is not. "

Carl G. Jung

Day 306

New Inner Life

Nothing you have manifested in your life is there without your agreement. Even the things you don't like. What you can change instantly is how you attend to these agreements. How you respond to a break-up, financial loss, problems with your health. Or how you respond to success, to the gifts you are receiving every day of your life, to your personal growth. That's the incredible power you already have: the way you respond. And to what you respond. Very soon, your outer life will reflect your new inner life. Manifestation, when you let go of all the luggage you have collected throughout life, becomes easier and easier.

Day 307

"Stop recreating the past, stop recreating the horrors of addiction. The pattern can be broken. It's your turn. You know recovery is your new pattern. Your new direction in life. Let this daily habit be of help. To build a new structure. A foundation for a new life. The past does not have to repeat itself. At the beginning of every day: stop for a moment. To focus on you. For a couple of minutes. To observe. To know that you're alive. To determine your direction and to be grateful. And then life is your reward." - 21 Exercises

DAY 308

What words of advice would you give to someone who is about to relapse?

DAY 309

LETTING GO

To help you further on your recovery journey it's good to focus on things that can support you. There are several ways to help you during this journey. Awakening, recovery is not about adding more things, but it is about letting go. Letting go of the lies you have told yourself of what you should have before you can be happy or successful, or receive love. No, you are already there. You are already worthy, loved, in union, certain. But through the stories we have told ourselves, society, the media, our upbringing has drowned us in, we have been separated from that truth. Awakening, therefore, is a journey of letting go. Go within and ask your higher self for support, ask the questions of what you need now to go further on this journey. For one it could be relaxing more, laughing more, for another to involve the mind by reading about these topics, or connecting to people who can support you. Write down a list of things that feel good to you. By writing it down you make it more definite. And much more likely that you more easily choose these things because they're now in your awareness.

DAY 310

"There is no such uncertainty as a sure thing." - Robert Burns

Day 311

CONTROL OVER YOUR CRAVING

Go over your pattern of addiction and then visualize until the early stages of actually acting out the behavior. Then, instead of drinking another glass, or placing another bet, visualize that you stop. For example, withdrawing your money from the sports betting site, pouring the wine in the sink, etc.

What this exercise does is to give you control over your craving. You are creating a limit for this behavior. Even if, for a moment it's in control, you're taking back the control almost immediately. No more hours of drinking, or gaming. But a swift, decisive break of the behavior. You can do the visualization sitting or lying down in a comfortable position, and, if you'd like, with music. It can take anywhere from 3 to 20 minutes.

Or longer if that feels right to you.

Day 312

"There is something truer and more real, than what we can see with the eyes, and touch with the finger."
Nathaniel Hawthorne

Day 313

Realize Your Purpose

Through mindfulness, you create a distance between you and addiction. In a relaxed state of mind, it's easier to let go of heavy, destructive thoughts. In this freedom, you can write your own story. I have been through this journey of hardship. All that I can tell is that overcoming addiction starts inside. And that a meditative state, a state of mindfulness, is the key to this inner journey. Here, in this inner world of mystery, you can create a new life of recovery. A new life of freedom and joy. To make that jump into the unknown. Away from the lies, and horrors of addiction.

To realize your purpose on this planet. Because life is so much more than fighting an addiction.

Day 314

"What you spend years creating, others could destroy overnight. Create anyway. If you find serenity and happiness, some may be jealous. Be happy anyway. The good you do today, will often be forgotten. Do good anyway. Give the best you have, and it will never be enough. Give your best anyway."

Mother Teresa

Day 315

Look in the mirror now, for three to five minutes straight. Set an alarm. Try not to stare, but to look. Then, reflect on it.

What did you see?

Day 316

Negative Repetitive Thought Patterns

Addiction recovery self-help is no longer the sole domain of people who are heavily addicted to alcohol, drugs, sex or gambling.

It has become wider, because people are waking up. Seeing that always having a lack of money is the cause of an addictive pattern, that being unhappily single is the cause of an addictive pattern, the list is endless.

Negative repetitive thought patterns, lead to destruction.

Day 317

Keep questioning the old continuously.
What is that no longer works.

Because the letting go of the old,
Is a prerequisite for the new to emerge fully.

And then, indeed, a new dawn is coming.

DAY 318

DELAYING OCCURRENCES

The ego, the lower mind at this moment is obstructing you. It is delaying occurrences.

So, rise beyond it. Do this by being silent.

By observing the thoughts, the worries, the emotions, and then see how it will disappear. As if it never even existed. It is just an illusion, all of what the ego and the lower mind is striving for.

Yes, you will need money, the concept of time, and so you will need your mind. But all will be servants. None of them will be masters. And they will be playing a far, far less important place as you are giving them now. The power is in *you*.. All is coming together. The time is now.

DAY 319

"A man who can't bear to share his habits
is a man who needs to quit them."

Stephen King, *The Dark Tower*

DAY 320

REALIZE YOUR PURPOSE

Your ideal vision and your goals are not written in stone. They can fluctuate and they should be organic, like all things in life. Things can occur that will impact your vision and goals. We can't control everything that's going on in our lives. It's paradoxical. You need to be very persistent and consistent when you want to achieve your goals in life, yet you also need to allow flexibility so that you can alter your life goals when circumstances change or your ever-changing interests demand a new course and new goals. You can always decide what you want in life.

DAY 321

Addiction may have dictated your past. But it's not invited to dictate your future. A brand new future is here, now. Embrace it.

Look forward. Take the steps into the unknown. You can do this. You are here for a reason. Addiction has nothing left to teach you. So transcend it. Thank it for all it has taught you. And then, let it go.

Let go.

Embrace the new.

DAY 322

WEEKLY REFLECTION

What one or two simple action(s) can you take this week to improve your relationship with yourself?

DAY 323

NOT PERFECT

There is no perfect recovery.

Everyone has their own road.

Their own 'rules'.

You know, deep within, what is good for you. What the right path is for you. So follow that inner voice. Don't be obsessed with being perfect. Do it as good as possible. Know that craving never brings the results you are after. That it never brings true reward. A true, genuine good feeling. So choose a direction that feels naturally to you. Stop the force.

Align to what is natural, what is authentic.

DAY 324

"It seems like a lifetime ago, the lies, the smell, the tears. But it was me. Drinking was my life. Now that I am seeing how beautiful life is on the other side, far away from addiction, miles away, I often ask myself from time to time, how could it be that I didn't quit earlier? Far away from addiction, miles away."

Joanne Edmund, *Happy & Sober*

Day 325

Keep Demanding Answers

We must make it our journey to uncover what is hidden beneath the surface.

The shadow within us.

That what is making us in conflict, drives us toward frustration, anger, craving, sadness. What is it that drives that darker side within us? Demand answers. When are you triggered? Why are you triggered? Why do you keep repeating thoughts, actions? Keep going, for better answers. To align with the truth. Your truth. The true you.

The authentic self.

Day 326

If you closely examine your worries, you'll see that they're mere thoughts. And sometimes accompanied by emotions, sensations in the body. Sit down for a moment and pay attention to what worries actually are. Become aware of what has such a gripping and disempowering effect on our lives.

DAY 327

REALIZE YOUR PURPOSE

What is wonderful about your life?

Why is your life a miracle?

To open our eyes to the beauty. To what is truly amazing. There is so much already here. So many desires that are already manifested one way or another. So many dreams that can be aligned to right now, by just taking a few steps in that direction. We make life complicated. With our thoughts. With comparison. But it is simple. Much simpler than we want to admit. Just be. And feel, hear, know the answers. The suffering is over: right here, right now. But there are days, hours, moments, where we lose the connection to who we really are. In these moments of frustration, or craving, or despair: wake up for a second. And be: be here, right now. To realize that the power is in each and every moment to transcend the suffering, just like that.

DAY 328

"Everybody knows if you are too careful you are so occupied in being careful that you are sure to stumble over something. "

Gertrude Stein

DAY 329

What feelings and thoughts are you suppressing?

What would happen with these feelings and thoughts in the coming year if you don't give yourself the time and space to express them?

Day 330

Find Your Own Safety

Find your own safety.

Addiction in many ways is a way to control.

To find some kind of peace. Some kind of relief.

To not confront. What's bothering you.

The feelings. This moment. To escape this very moment.

I dare you: confront it, what is so scary?

That we try to find so many,

elaborate and destructive ways to avoid it?

Day 331

Why should you be the one running after things?

Chasing things?

Why not turn the tables?

Determine what attracts what.

Then be the one who is attracted.

Zen Mirrors

Day 332

It's What You Deserve

Let's go forward.

Let's dissolve, transcend what has been.

What is running you subconsciously.

The time has come.

To decide.

Your own way.

Your own path.

Your own direction.

Somewhere, far away, but oh so close, is your destiny.

Walk now. Walk towards what you know to be true.

Because it's what you deserve.

More than anything, it's what you deserve.

Day 333

"When you do things from your soul,
you feel a river moving in you, a joy."

Rumi

DAY 334

GRATITUDE

Sometimes it's hard to remember the full blessing we receive every day. Take a moment. And look around you. Look within. See the past. The dinners, the walks, the smiles, the kiss. All what you've been blessed with through this lifetime. And all that's surrounding you now.

Take a moment. To breathe it in.
The gifts, the gifts of life.

DAY 335

Don't feel too bad about feeling lonely. Or loneliness. But feel it. Welcome it. It's part of the feelings of a human existence. And be assured, it's not the end. This feeling too will pass. Times will change.

So I say to you, embrace the loneliness whenever you are feeling it. And on the other hand, enjoy this feeling, these moments of being alone. This too will pass.

So make the most out of it now. You never know what comes next. So enjoy moments while they last.

DAY 336

WEEKLY REFLECTION

What do you find most difficult about your relationship with yourself? Write down one or two ways to improve this.

DAY 337

FIND YOUR OWN SAFETY

Allow yourself to believe that the Creator, God, The Universe has heard your intentions. When spoken from the heart. From your authentic self. And that you will receive valuable insights along the way. That it will come to you in surprising ways.

So rather than picking apart, feeling anxious, and wanting to control every step of the way:

Feel excitement for what is about to come!

Be surprised. Let The Universe work it's magic. And be flexible. So you can tweak your intention, your desired manifestation, when the circumstances of your life changes.

DAY 338

"Our ego and mind are always turning to history for information. It works backwards. The intuition and your visionary self is leading you into the future. Towards the vision. So that you can learn, you can grow."

Lee Harris

DAY 339

IT'S WHAT YOU DESERVE

If you want to quit a not-working relationship, try to first heal your false predictions about the other within. Heal what is broken within. Heal, or accept, or make the best of it before moving on. Then the chances of attracting these kinds of relationships, or persons in your life again, will diminish hugely.

DAY 340

Your body is your companion during this lifetime. It helps you to move, to see, to hear, to feel, to experience. And it knows the truth. The phrase, *Your body's a temple,* becomes true when you really, closely pay attention. It's an easy test. If you have a dilemma right now, ask yourself the question. For example, *Shall I continue with my study or not?* And then sit down in silence. First feel how your body reacts to answer a, *I want to continue my study.* Then to the other answer. You will feel in the body what's most true to you.

In that way the question, *What does your body try to tell you in the past few months?* Becomes a very important question. Because the body knows. So play close attention to this trusted companion.

DAY 341

ONLY IN SILENCE A NEW FUTURE CAN BE FOUND

All thoughts (mind) can be traced back to fear.

Your thoughts don't want to change, and any impulse that breeds change is stopped by the mind. One way or another. The mind is linked to the comfort zone. The mind serves you with thoughts that support your current beliefs.

Other thoughts, radical new thoughts are blocked, or ridiculed For fear of change. Your current thoughts will therefore only contribute to a future that is possible for your mind to see.

Only in silence a new future can be found.

DAY 342

"Drop the idea of becoming someone,
because you are already a masterpiece.
You cannot be improved.
You have only to come to it, to know it, to realize it."

Osho

DAY 343

What is your most powerful habit and why? What is another simple but powerful action you can turn into a habit?

Day 344

Find Your Own Safety

Thoughts assume the worst, the worst-case scenario for the future. So that we take safety precautions against imaginary painful consequences.

This keeps us within our comfort zone. No change.

Besides that, assuming the worst in the future means that you suffer in the now about something that has not yet happened and of which, realistically, it is also very doubtful whether it actually will happen.

Day 345

"Self growth begins with knowing what you want. What's your direction in life? We sometimes feel the pressure to make something out of our lives—and that's normal. However, without a clear direction, stress comes in and it's hard to ignore. What do I want from my brief time on this Earth? Our lives never stay the same permanently. Peaks and valleys, remember? While fluctuation in life is normal, you don't want to catch yourself in a downward spiral for decades, years, or even months. Take matters into your own hands and determine your course." - 21 Exercises

DAY 346

COMMUNICATION

Isn't communication, words, not the source of so many problems? To say what you truly want to say. The words that you need to say. The questions you need to ask. The answers you want to give. Both in the communication with others, as in the communication with ourselves we often lack sincerity. Or, rather, the courage to communicate with sincerity. It's good to be aware of your own communication. Why do you say the things you say? And why don't you say the things you want to say? What's happening when you communicate with others, and what is happening when you communicate with others?

Examine yourself. Pay close attention, and a richer more enjoyable life is your reward.

DAY 347

"There exists only the present instant...
a Now which always and without end is itself new.
There is no yesterday nor any tomorrow, but only Now,
as it was a thousand years ago
and as it will be a thousand years hence."
Meister Eckhart

DAY 348

What money beliefs do you hold?

Both the love for money as the lack of money create drastic problems. To find out what money is we need to go back to the source. The paper, the coins, the numbers on an online account. It's perceived value. It has no 'real' value, the paper, the coins, the numbers.

From a spiritual viewpoint money is neutral, it's energy. Examine your relationship with money, what patterns are repeating itself when it comes to your financial situation? Realize that, with the neutral nature of money, you can do both creative things with it, as well as destructive. Build a swimming pool, destroy a forest.

Money problems therefore, have everything to do with how you perceive it. With what kind of financial situation you subconsciously align yourself.

DAY 349

"Nobody can hurt me without my permission." - Mahatma Gandhi

DAY 350

What patterns keep repeating themselves in your life when it comes to money?

Day 351

What negative money beliefs do you hold? And how can you rephrase these beliefs into something more empowering?

Day 352

What does money represent for you? And write down how this is already present in your life. For example: *Money means safety to me. Safety is already in my life, I have a home, a stable job, good health.*

DAY 353

TWO CREATIONS

Everything in life has two creations.

We are all familiar with the second creation - the buildings around you, great sporting victories, an outstanding movie. But before this actual creation, there is the first creation. An idea, a thought, an instinct, that is made into a plan and set into motion. Sometimes it doesn't take more than a couple of seconds. You see an incredibly attractive person, you'll notice a tingling feeling and maybe approach this person. Within those milliseconds, between feeling and walking up to this attractive stranger and actually starting to talk, there is a decision. That decision has the potential to change your life.

If you look at your own life, how many of these potentially life-changing decisions are waiting to be made?

DAY 354

"It's amazing how lovely common things become, if one only knows how to look at them."

Louisa May Alcott

Day 355

Deepen Your Experience

To deepen your connection with your soul, with life, will help you to deepen your experience day-by-day. See lessons where you didn't see them before.

It helps you to stop running around in circles, chasing the same patterns over and again. Letting go of what you don't need. Especially letting go of thoughts, worries, and fear.

The road, the journey of life will stay bumpy, but when your roots are more stable, dealing with life becomes more natural. More joyful too. More effortless. Like in a *flow*. Like a river, like water.

Day 356

"Hope is the thing with feathers
That perches in the soul
And sings the tune without the words
And never stops at all."

Emily Dickinson

Day 357

Weekly Reflection

Write down an empowering response to the addiction thought:

I will never be free from addiction.

Day 358

Roses

"Pay attention, open your eyes in truth, and be adaptable to what life is asking from you moment to moment. What you felt one moment to be true, can be different in the next. Stop being stubborn. But float with the natural changing character of life. Go for your goals, your intention in full. Without attachment. Don't close your eyes. But see with new ones. Perceive the truth with noble acceptance. Embrace your intention, embrace the magnificent uncertainty of all. The gift of not knowing, means you can be surprised at each moment. The curtains opening, again and again. Say yes to that flow. Have faith in your being. Find your roots, and as roses dance in the wind of thousand changes."

Zen Mirrors

Day 359

It's time to realize your accomplishments. From which point did you start this book, and where are you now?

Hold still for a moment. Be with your accomplishment. Your lessons. The movement of life.

DAY 360

Write down at least three accomplishments you have achieved this year, and why it's an important accomplishment for you.

DAY 361

Write down the two or three most important lessons you've learned this year.

DAY 362

FIND YOUR SONG

Whenever the hardship comes in, the shadow falls, be assured that that sparkle of light, even if it shines in the faraway distance, can be enough to break through, to change, to take a turn for the better.

DAY 363

Realize you've come here, to this earth, to this one life, with a purpose, a calling. There is a song waiting within you. You have the voice, the being, the qualities to sing that song. To follow your music. Your calling. To make your life a ride of joy, a ride of discovery, a ride of creation, a ride of love. To make this experience truly worthwhile. Don't play the level of craving over and over again. It's not worth it. There is life after addiction. There is life after recovery. There is so much more out there for you to discover. Embrace it. Embrace the new. Empty the old. The beliefs, the stories, the thoughts that clearly don't work. Replace them.

Write a new chapter.

Walk a new path.

Find your song.

And start singing it.

DAY 364

IT HAS BEEN

Through sadness and tears, there shines a small and ever glowing light.
The dark days have been and will be, but never it is dark enough to dim the light.
It's in you.
It's above you.
It's around you.

A faraway cry, echoing in the dark,
A child, a teenager, a you lost in time, alone, someplace, somewhere. But time, being a strange thing, goes back and forth.
Now you, strong, brave and full of life gives your hand to her, to him, lonesome waiting in the past.
A kind word, an arm wrapped around your shoulder brings you back to the present.

It has been, it has been.

DAY 365

Write a letter to yourself, to be opened one year from now.

This Has Been:

OVERCOME ADDICTION

365 INSPIRATIONS FOR RECOVERY

If you want to focus on becoming free from addiction & commit to recovery every day, follow my instagram account. With a recovery inspiration every day.

Instagram: become_recovery

https://www.instagram.com/become_recovery/.

Printed in Great Britain
by Amazon

81003621R00133